the
ANTI-INFLAMMATION COOKBOOK

the ANTI-INFLAMMATION COOKBOOK

The Delicious Way to Reduce Inflammation and Stay Healthy

AMANDA HAAS

WITH DR. BRADLY JACOBS

PHOTOGRAPHS BY ERIN KUNKEL

CHRONICLE BOOKS
SAN FRANCISCO

Designed by Sara Schneider

Food styling by George Dolese and Elizabet Nederlanden

Prop styling by Glenn Jenkins

Ancient Harvest is a registered trademark of Quinoa Corporation.
Annie Chun's is a registered trademark of CJ Cheiljedang Corporation.
Benadryl is a registered trademark of Johnson & Johnson.
Bionature is a registered trademark of Archer Daniels Midland Company.
Bob's Red Mill is a registered trademark of Bob's Red Mill Natural Foods, Inc.
Cup4Cup is a registered trademark of Elizabeth M LLC.
Equal is a registered trademark of the Merisant Company.
Host Defense is a registered trademark of Stamets, Paul DBA Fungi Perfecti.
Microplane is a registered trademark of Grace Manufacturing Inc.
Splenda is a registered trademark of Johnson & Johnson.
Sweet'N Low is a registered trademark of CPC Intellectual Property, Inc.
Thai Kitchen is a registered trademark of Simply Asia Foods, Inc.
Tylenol is a registered trademark of Johnson & Johnson.
Udi's is a registered trademark of Udi's Healthy Foods, LLC.
Vegenaise is a registered trademark of Old Friend's Holdings, LLC.

Chronicle books and gifts are available at special quantity discounts to corporations, professional associations, literacy programs, and other organizations. For details and discount information, please contact our premiums department at corporatesales@chroniclebooks.com or at 1-800-759-0190.

10 9 8 7 6 5 4 3 2

Chronicle Books LLC
680 Second Street
San Francisco, California 94107
www.chroniclebooks.com

"Tell me what you eat and I'll tell you what you are."

— Jean Anthelme Brillat-Savarin

CONTENTS

ACKNOWLEDGMENTS

This is my favorite part of cookbook writing. I get to thank all the people who enable me to chase my dream career, including

Lorena Jones, my editor at Chronicle Books: From Day One, you got me. You knew what I wanted this book to be, and made it come to life long before we shook on it. Thank you for your commitment to me and this topic.

Dr. Bradly Jacobs: I am so fortunate that Lorena connected us. You have already improved my quality of life, and will help so many others through this book. Thank you so much.

The entire team at Chronicle Books: Creative director and designer Sara Schneider, production developer Tera Killip, production designer Steve Kim, and managing editor Doug Ogan. I couldn't ask for a better team to bring my vision to life in print.

Erin Kunkel: Erin, it's like you took my vision out of my head and put it in front of your lens. What an incredible talent you are. I can't wait to do it again.

George Dolese: Words aren't enough for you, my friend. You figured out exactly what I wanted and cooked it into reality. Thank you for taking so much pride in this project and for allowing me into your world for the week. You're the best.

Elisabet der Nederlanden: Watching you and George work together is like watching an orchestra perform—you move flawlessly together. Thank you for preparing such beautiful food.

Glenn Jenkins: Glenn, your keen eye and incredible taste in tabletop brought this book to life. Thank you for finding the perfect everything to make each shot beautiful.

Carole Bidnick, my agent: Thank you so much for your commitment to this book.

Tori Ritchie, my mentor and the one who believes in me the most: You are the reason I get to do this for a living. Thank you for sharing your faith in me with others. You are a trusted friend and an inspiration!

My Family at Williams-Sonoma: I get to work for the company I love while continuing my love of cookbook writing. I'm hoarding all the best food jobs in the world! Thank you, Laura Alber, Janet Hayes, Neil Lick, Shane Brogan, Jean Armstrong, and everyone else I work with. And to my amazing test-kitchen team, Sandra Wu, Melissa Stewart, and Amanda Frederickson, thank you for working so hard in our test kitchen and testing for me at home. I'm so lucky to work with you three. And thank you to our founder, Chuck Williams. Without you, American cooking would not be what it is today. You are an inspiration to me and millions of others.

Inken Chrisman: My work wife, my supporter, my right-hand woman . . . you are truly amazing. This book would not have happened without your discipline and testing skills.

Jodi Liano: You, too, have become a trusted advisor and inspiration. I love the work we get to do together.

Chef Todd English: Thank you for the continual reminder that I was meant to do this work. I love our shared belief that cooking for others is the absolute best job in the world!

Kate Leahy: This book never would have gotten off the ground without your way with words. Thank you so much for fine-tuning my proposal.

Others: There are so many amazing cooks and chefs I've been lucky enough to meet, but several continue to inspire me—Katherine Cobbs, Mary Risley, Matthew Accarrino, Michael Mina, Mourad Lahlou, Shelley Lindgren, Tyler Florence, Ben Jacobsen, and my favorite home cooks, my girlfriends.

Last but certainly not least, thanks to my awesome family: Kyle, thank you for all of the effort and time you give our children so I can do this work every day. Charlie, I love cooking with you! You inspire me in the kitchen every day. You are a cooking star. Connor, you make me want to cook. Thank you for always being the most gracious and appreciative eater at the table. You three are the reason I do all of this. And Mom and Dad, thank you so much for making food a part of my life. (Was there ever any doubt I'd pursue eating for a living?) I love you all.

PREFACE

by Dr. Bradly Jacobs

I went into medicine to treat the whole person and was deeply motivated to understand my patients in the context of their personal life experiences, which requires listening attentively to their life stories, learning about their family lives, recognizing the early symptoms and triggers, and understanding how stress, food, exercise, sleep, relationships, and finding purpose all influence their lives.

Although my medical-school professors would like to have convinced me otherwise, I learned from years of martial-arts study that we are energetic bodies, not limited to flesh, bone, and blood, and that we are capable of self-renewal. As a teenager, I recall my grandmother saying, "If you don't have your health, you don't have anything. . . . No amount of power or money can counter poor health." In 1989, as a second-year medical student at Stanford University, I came to appreciate this truth firsthand when my healthy, fifty-year-old father suddenly developed difficulty finding his words and was subsequently diagnosed with a malignant brain tumor called a glioblastoma multiforme.

Through personal loss, I learned from the inside out when and how to apply conventional medical therapies (such as medications, procedures, and surgery), alternative medicine therapies (such as acupuncture and herbal medicine), and lifestyle therapies (such as nutrition, mind-body therapies, exercise, and cultivating quality relationships).

Based on these life experiences, I became committed to expanding my medical training to become a more well-rounded and effective physician (the word *doctor* has the same Latin root as *teacher*), one with a grasp of disciplines and perspectives other than what I had learned in medical school. In so doing, I hoped to become a better healer, listener, and communicator. Two of the most important topics I studied were nutritional and functional medicine. I learned the profound role that food plays in maintaining our health.

I have spent the past fifteen years caring for thousands of people with a vast range of health issues, including cancer, cardiovascular conditions (stroke and heart attack), autoimmune conditions (inflammatory bowel disease, sprue, multiple sclerosis, lupus, and type 1 diabetes), and lifestyle-related diseases (type 2 diabetes, osteoarthritis, elevated cholesterol, generalized anxiety, and sleep disturbances). Despite the diversity of conditions and health issues, a couple irreconcilable truths emerged: "upstream events" (factors that have occurred before a person seeks medical treatment) matter, and lifestyle modifications can have a profoundly positive effect.

A set of upstream events appears to cause each person's seemingly different medical conditions, for example, high blood pressure or sprue. Some of these factors are modifiable by changing lifestyle, environment, or both; others, resulting from family history, childhood/early adult exposures, travel-related events, and genetic mutations, are not.

Modifiable factors, such as lifestyle (diet, activity, stress, sleep, and tobacco use) and environment (exposure to infectious agents, toxins, and pollutants, and community safety) have a dramatic impact on health and well-being. Research has demonstrated that lifestyle choices can prevent more than 55 percent of deaths each year. Put very simply, with every vegetable serving eaten daily, the risk of dying of any cause is reduced by about 6 percent per year. These modifiable factors are the magic pill that we all are looking for.

Put into practice, here's how considering the effects of upstream events and modifiable factors influenced one patient's care: It was a warm autumn day in September. I had completed my general internal medicine residency and research fellowship at the University of California, San Francisco (UCSF), and begun seeing patients as assistant clinical professor and founding medical director for the UCSF Osher Center for Integrative Medicine.

One of the first patients I worked with at the Osher Center was Maria. The thirty-four-year-old mother of two toddlers had experienced two years of chronic intermittent abdominal pain, headaches, light-headedness, bouts of shortness of breath, muscle aches, and "brain fog." Her previous general internal medicine doctor had worked diligently to assign a diagnosis to these complaints, to no avail. In the search for an answer to the underlying causes of her seemingly disparate complaints, she had seen a neurologist, endocrinologist, cardiologist, rheumatologist, pulmonologist, and gastroenterologist. She had undergone CT scans of her abdomen and chest, MRI scans of her brain, endoscopy, colonoscopy, small bowel follow-through, echocardiography, tilt table testing, pulmonary function testing, and myriad laboratory tests. Unfortunately for Maria, despite the extensive work-up and brainpower of this collection of well-meaning physicians, no diagnosis had been given. Each referring specialist would write something similar to this: "All tests are negative. Her complaints are not related to my area of specialization."

Maria would not take "we don't know" for an answer and began going to the emergency room during episodes when her symptoms escalated. During one of these visits, she complained of feeling anxious and depressed (understandably) as a result of her symptoms, at which point she received an evaluation by a psychiatrist, who appropriately stated that she was suffering from situational anxiety and depression. Once the words *depression* and *anxiety* were inscribed in the medical chart, it became much easier for the admittedly frustrated physicians to ascribe her symptoms to being "all in her head."

Consequently, her primary care doctor prescribed antidepressant and antianxiety medications, and her specialist doctors then were able to assign her symptoms to the "nonphysical" domain of "depression and anxiety," thus getting them off the hook for continuing the search for a root cause of her complaints. Since she still had physical pain, she was prescribed pain medications, which led to dependence problems. At that moment, the tremendous collective energy and resources dedicated to finding the answer ceased. No longer were doctors interested in doing further diagnostic testing, let alone going back to square one and listening carefully to her story.

I had the advantage of seeing Maria after she had undergone a full battery of diagnostic tests and seen nearly a dozen doctors. After reviewing her medical chart, I realized that no one had asked her about her life experience prior to developing these symptoms. In preparation for my visit with Maria, I decided that I would ask her to tell me her story and would give her as much time as she needed to recount her life experience. In the first forty minutes of our visit, I learned that her mother had told her she had "stomach problems" ever since she was a kid.

Maria remembered becoming friendly with the school nurse because she would visit her so frequently in elementary school, most often within an hour after lunch recess. Her mother was a "health nut," so her breakfast was usually cereal or eggs, and lunches consisted of peanut butter and jelly or tuna sandwiches on whole-wheat bread, or whole-wheat pasta with tomato sauce. She can remember one summer in Hawaii, when her stomach complaints and headaches vanished. Her mother reasoned that her environment was causing problems, but her symptoms didn't seem to improve when she traveled to visit their relatives in the Midwest. In college, her doctors considered celiac disease, but her tests came back "negative," and she was told that was not her problem. By the end of our visit, it became clear that food had been a major trigger to her symptoms, and she agreed to try an elimination diet for one month.

Within three months, Maria discovered that wheat, oats, tomatoes, and eggplant were the culprits for 90 percent of her symptoms. After I prescribed a modified diet, probiotics, select nutrients, and mind-body therapies, she no longer required pain medication. After six months, she was off antidepressants and living what she called a normal life.

Although we have long recognized the importance of food in promoting good health, only in the past ten years have we come to appreciate how food can *damage* our health. The industrialization of food production has successfully modified foundational food products like grains and meats in ways that render them novel foodstuffs to our highly evolved digestive tract and the bacteria within it. As a result, some people experience unanticipated changes in the normal function of their digestive tract in the immune response to foods considered staples in our ancestors' diets. Consequently, people are experiencing myriad seemingly unrelated symptoms like headaches, fatigue, and joint pain.

Amanda Haas's life experience is similar to Maria's and countless others who have seen too many doctors and undergone too many diagnostic tests, only to be given a wrong diagnosis or to be told that the symptoms are "all in their heads."

While many people are able to eat a full range of food types without problems, other people experience symptoms that, while minor for some, may be severe and disabling for them. Often, disabling symptoms are the result of multiple events, such as genetic mutations combined with an infection compounded by persistent exposure to foods that cause inflammation for that individual. Thankfully, Amanda has found her path to wellness and imparts her wisdom as a gifted professional cook, providing us with delicious recipes based on the ingredients that will engender improved health as well as a happy palate.

Together, we hope to provide you with insight into how to use specific ingredients to get certain nutrients you may be lacking and to guide you to the ingredients and recipes that will help you better manage symptoms and conditions that are affected by inflammation. Here's to using food as your path to living a vibrant, joyful, and long life.

MY STORY

by Amanda Haas

The joke in my family is that I look healthy. The truth is I've been sick all my life. Allergies, asthma, eczema, and back spasms have sidelined me since childhood. Apparent "stomach bugs" have landed me in the hospital more than half a dozen times. Chronic heartburn, endless stomach pain, and bouts of sudden nausea arrived about a decade ago. The final straw was six years ago, when I contracted parvovirus—a fairly innocuous virus for children but often havoc wreaking on adults. A rheumatologist explained I was one of the unlucky ones. The virus latched on to me and wouldn't let go, leaving me with symptoms of rheumatoid arthritis. Day in, day out, I'd be hurting all over and feeling like a hypochondriac. Every year since, I've woken up on New Year's Day vowing to figure out my health problems in the year ahead.

I have tried everything to find a cure for my pain, ranging from Western medical treatments to alternative healing practices. My contact list reads like a who's who of the health treatment world: acupuncturist, massage therapist, rheumatologist, gastroenterologist, allergist, orthopedist, physical therapist, osteopath, and even my dad (psychiatrist). When I had a second flare-up of the virus in 2010, blood work showed that my sedimentation rate (SED)—a measure of inflammation in the body—was significantly elevated. I finally agreed to let my rheumatologist start me on a traditional yet depressing routine of steroids and rheumatoid arthritis drugs, including a big ol' shot I had to give myself biweekly and a pill form of chemotherapy. My SED rate dropped, but I still hurt like crazy. That's when I decided to get one more opinion.

In 2011, I walked into an allergist's office at the end of my rope. As I sat there in tears, I listed my litany of problems. I explained how I'd tested negative for celiac disease even though I had a hunch that gluten was the cause of my heartburn and stomach problems. I showed him the drugs I was taking. He sat patiently and asked me question after question, including what I did for a living. When I told him I was a cook and recipe developer, his eyes lit up like a Christmas tree. He pointed out that my list of ailments read like a catalog of inflammatory disease–related issues. (This was good news?) Then, he asked me the most obvious question of all: If food was my life, why hadn't I looked to it for the answers?

If I had been listening to my gut—as I have done for most of my crucial life decisions—I would have known that what I was eating was my problem. Yet I feared that examining my food intake would make my life less enjoyable. Or that it could sideline my career working with chefs and others in the food industry. I also thought I couldn't afford all the supplements and foods I'd need to make changes. After explaining the different types of gluten reactions, my allergist sent me away with strict instructions: Remove all gluten from my diet, see how I felt, and start reading up on the connection between inflammation and food.

Eliminating gluten made an incredible difference. I saw an astounding improvement in my health. The stomach pain, vomiting, heartburn, and, most remarkably, back spasms subsided immediately. I was able to get off my medications. I felt so much better, that I didn't even miss my favorite foods. After getting over the self-consciousness of telling coworkers I had become gluten-free (it was impossible not to sound like I was hopping on the latest diet trend), I began looking beyond gluten to understand the foods that cause inflammation and the foods that fight it. I read everything I could get my hands on, from studies by experts on inflammation to nutritionists who use food to heal patients.

I became enthralled with the personal success stories I heard anytime I'd mention to friends my curiosity about the relationship between diet and inflammation. Avoiding gluten was the first necessary change for me, but for someone who loves food as much as I do, I was reticent to remove other categories of food from my diet. Like many others, I use food for comfort and relaxation and can easily overdo it. Although I was no longer sick to my stomach or having back spasms, I'd wake up frequently with joint pain, headaches, and general back pain. I finally realized that my pain always occurred after a big meal. Again, my gut was trying to tell me something. I was doing better, but I still had work to do.

That's when I decided to write this book. I realized that if I could create recipes that stave off inflammation, I would literally cook my way out of pain and into a healthier, happier life. I informed my family that we were going to shake things up, but I promised them that my food would still taste great. As I began work on this project, I was lucky enough to be connected with Dr. Bradly Jacobs. After a long conversation about my health, he supported my health-improvement plan and agreed to partner with me on this book. We worked together to identify the foods that were causing my symptoms of back and joint pain and fatigue.

My first step was to empty my pantry of the clearly documented trigger foods and replace them with alternatives. I reined in my bacon habit and worked hard to make sure processed foods were a very small part of my diet. I made more space in my refrigerator for fresh produce and proteins. I reduced my alcohol intake. Plus, to stay true to my mantra that you can cook delicious food on a budget, I insisted on sticking to one.

This book shares what I learned as I cooked my way back to health, and how I eliminated the foods that were causing me pain, while creating delicious, simple recipes that calmed my inflammation. By finally trusting my instincts and listening to my gut, I turned to better habits in the kitchen that also made me a better cook. In turn, I have more energy than ever, and my sons have started lists of *their* new favorite recipes. Though I have been a professional cook for nearly two decades, the discoveries and practices in this book have become the most meaningful work of my career so far.

Even if you don't have life-altering symptoms, as I did, but simply want to lower your level of systemic inflammation for general wellness, the information and ideas here will improve the quality of your life when you understand how the right whole foods can be the best medicine for you and how delicious such healing cooking can be.

ABOUT INFLAMMATION

At its most basic, inflammation is the body's response to outside irritants and stresses. Inflammation is a natural part of our immune system, and without it our wounds wouldn't heal. But when inflammation becomes chronic, it upsets the natural balance of our internal ecosystems, wrecking havoc on our digestive and nervous systems. Innumerable factors bring on chronic inflammation, and more and more people are becoming aware of its effects, electing to eliminate known irritants, such as gluten, in an effort to feel better. Yet while gluten sensitivity has gone mainstream, gluten is not the only irritant causing chronic inflammation. The typical Western diet of processed foods, excessive sugar, regular alcohol consumption, and too little of the foods that naturally counter inflammation, such as fresh vegetables, seeds, nuts, and oily fish, is contributing greatly to widespread chronic inflammation.

Chronic inflammation can prompt or worsen diseases such as heart disease, inflammatory diseases (i.e., rheumatoid arthritis, lupus, celiac disease), diabetes, or many others (the list is long) At its lesser effect, chronic inflammation can manifest as gastrointestinal upset, lethargy, or overall malaise. You'll see cancer frequently referenced in the information about beneficial and problematic foods. Put very simply, cancer loves inflammation, so reducing systemic levels of inflammation can be one way to positively manage or possibly prevent cancer. As a first step, informed, intentional eating can play a material role in promoting overall wellness and curbing the onset or progression of diseases that are negatively affected by inflammation.

— oxidation and inflammation —

Oxidative stress results from an inability of antioxidants (for example, superoxide dismutase, glutathione, vitamin C, and vitamin D) to sufficiently eliminate waste products (such as free radicals and reactive metabolites) that are typically generated during the normal cellular energy production process. Under chronic stress conditions, our bodies have both increased demand to generate energy and decreased capacity to repair the body, which results in a chronic inflammatory state. Examples of food-based sources of chronic stress on the body include exposure to pesticides and herbicides, trigger foods, high-calorie and added-sugar diets, and alcohol consumption. Chronic health problems, particularly autoimmune conditions (such as inflammatory bowel disease, Crohn's, ulcerative colitis, diabetes, fibromyalgia, chronic fatigue syndrome, rheumatoid arthritis, and lupus), also have this effect.

— the digestive tract is key to improved health —

Although the digestive tract is inside the body, it is readily accessed by the outside world because the gastrointestinal lining is regularly exposed to billions of chemicals, organisms, and nutrients through the food and drink that we consume daily. Therefore, you can understand the importance of maintaining good gut health. Research has demonstrated that microorganisms living in our gastrointestinal tract not only influence our ability to digest and absorb food properly and regulate bowel function but also regulate other pathways, including the body's immune system development and function and vascular system, as well as its inflammatory and oxidative pathways.

As it turns out, poor gut health affects just about every organ, bodily system, and condition, and conversely better gut health can meaningfully improve a range of autoimmune conditions as well as diabetes, obesity, chronic back pain, and migraines. Some conventional practitioners may consider these improvements unrelated or spontaneous cures, but more of them are incorporating this thinking into their patient care.

Meet with your health-care practitioner to determine what you should be monitoring and recording, which diagnostic tests you should consider, and what modifications you might make in the short term. Ask for sources of reliable information on new findings relevant to your specific variables. Establish a timeline for exploration and assessment. Determine your immediate and long-term goals for treatment. If you are not yet working with a health-care provider, you can use a four-step process to help you identify potential triggers and patterns that perpetuate, worsen, or improve how well you feel.

— the 4R program —

The 4R Program is a diagnostic and guidance tool that is useful for the vast majority of people living with chronic disease. Designed for gut health, it is adapted from a program originally developed by Jeffrey Bland, PhD, at the Institute for Functional Medicine, and is a variant of the naturopathic approach called the 3R Program. Each "R" stands for a step in the process.

remove

Remove from your diet all foods that may have toxins; for example, dietary supplements that contain high heavy-metal content, fish from known or potentially polluted waters, and corn-fed meat raised on antibiotics and growth hormones.

Remove all foods to which your body reacts poorly—that is, those you notice don't agree with you. These include foods to which you seem to have a sensitivity. For example, remove dairy if you experience symptoms of lactose intolerance or wheat if you suffer from the effects associated with gluten intolerance whenever you consume these products. Remove all foods with added (not naturally occurring) sugar, artificial colors, and preservatives.

Eliminate irritants to the gut lining, such as coffee, alcohol, and nonsteroidal anti-inflammatory medications.

When the natural gut flora becomes unbalanced—which can disrupt nutrient absorption and/or cause persistent low-grade inflammation, restoring the natural balance is essential. Such imbalance can range from mild to severe and has a multitude of causes. Similarly, symptoms can be mild or severe, ranging from mild gastrointestinal (GI) upset to severe malabsorption, sometimes requiring hospitalization.

replace and supplement

The second "R" stands for Replace and Supplement and refers to people who have a diminished capacity to make digestive enzymes. Pancreatic insufficiency, as it is termed, leads to an inability to digest food and absorb nutrients and often is associated with bloating, gas, and general stomach discomfort. Using digestive enzyme replacements or stimulating stomach acids (another key to digestion) with betaine Houttuynia cordata injections (HCl) or herbal bitters are excellent remedies.

reinoculate and restore

The third step is to rebalance the microbiome in the digestive tract to ensure that health-promoting bacteria predominate over potentially harmful microbes. Go slowly when replacing the healthy bacteria to avoid gas formation and gut cramping. Start by consuming foods with 3 billion colony-forming units (CFU) daily and escalating to 15 billion CFU of healthy bacteria (lactobacillus and bifidobacteria species) or yeast (saccharomyces boulardii) daily. Foods should serve as your primary source. Look for foods in containers with the "Live & Active Cultures" seal, established by the National Yogurt Association, the industry's nonprofit trade organization in the United States. The seal indicates that a refrigerated product has at least 100 million cultures per gram and that a frozen product has at least 10 million cultures per gram. Remember to read the label to ensure there is substantially more than the minimum before purchasing.

Kefir, another source of CFU, has an enriched group of organisms, including bacteria and yeast. Because kefir undergoes a fermentation process, very little lactose remains, and therefore lactose-intolerant people tolerate kefir well. Sauerkraut and kimchi are other excellent sources. These foods are thought not only to inoculate the gut with healthful bacteria but to provide additional food (called fructo-oligosaccharide and inulin) for the bacteria already living in your gut, thereby improving the health and numbers of the existing healthy bacteria.

Reserve dietary supplements for days when you need to augment your consumption of whole foods in order to achieve your ideal CFU intake. When deciding which brand to purchase, look for those that have a third-party quality assurance seal of approval by the National Science Foundation or the U.S. Pharmacopeial Convention.

You will notice positive changes in your bowel consistency, bowel frequency, and bowel symptoms when you are getting adequate quantities and types of healthy microflora from your foods or dietary supplements. Regardless of what the packaging says, trust your gut reaction!

repair of intestinal lining

After two to three weeks of reinoculation, it's time to heal the lining of the gut. For a minimum of 90 days, take 1 to 3 g fish oil, 10 mg zinc, 6 g each of the amino acids glycine and l-glutamine, and 1 g pantothenic acid. This will effectively restore the inner lining of the gut, enabling it to digest and absorb nutrients and diminish absorption of foreign or toxic compounts that cause inflammation.

With this overview in mind, let's turn to the kitchen and survey the foods that are central to improvement.

THE ANTI-INFLAMMATORY KITCHEN

When attempting to improve your health through food, it's important to understand a few things: There are foods that cause inflammation, foods that reduce it, and many foods that do some of both or neither. After admitting that I needed to be more intentional about what I was consuming, I took a close look at my pantry. Instead of telling myself I'd just have this or that in small doses, I decided to *completely* remove the ingredients that made me feel lousy and replace them with ingredients that made me feel great. Once I took this step, I came to see how much better I felt very quickly, and I stopped thinking about the foods I would no longer have in my diet.

— a note about organics —

Yes, organic foods cost more than their nonorganic counterparts. However, after digging deep into the effects of regularly consuming pesticides and other toxic chemicals, I'm committed to buying organic foods as much as my budget allows. If you're looking to switch over to organics, I recommend starting with buying organic versions of apples and soft-skinned fruits. In the United States, these fruits are often referred to as the "dirty dozen," the twelve fruits and vegetables that absorb the most pesticides during the production cycle (listed in order from worst offender to least worrisome). Because different countries' farming and pesticide practices vary greatly, investigate local practices, identify the most concerning crops, and prioritize purchasing organics of the foods that have the most pesticide exposure.

apples	sweet bell peppers
strawberries	nectarines
grapes	cucumbers
celery	cherry tomatoes
peaches	snap peas (when imported)
spinach	potatoes

— feel-good foods—

The following foods include all the basics that make me feel healthy. I cook with these weekly. Some have proven anti-inflammatory properties and others are elemental to well-being. These are the foods that fulfill our caloric intake needs and also make us feel great. You'll see these ingredients—such as quinoa and eggs—used heavily throughout this book. They're all readily available at grocery stores everywhere.

ANIMAL PROTEINS:
GRASS-FED ORGANIC CHICKEN, PORK, LAMB, AND BEEF

Organic and grass-fed free-range animals are healthier, and their meat offers you better nutritional value and causes less harm than that of conventionally raised animals. Pasture-raised chickens, pigs, lambs, and cows have higher levels of omega-3 fatty acid (an anti-inflammatory fat) and lower levels of omega-6 fatty acid (a pro-inflammatory fat) compared with corn-fed animals. Not surprisingly, research shows a lower occurrence of disease is correlated with eating meat from grass-fed animals than from those that are corn-fed.

There are other health benefits of buying certified organic meats whenever possible, or at least meat that is certified to be without growth hormones or antibiotics. Hormone and antibiotic compounds that are fed to animals show up in the meat and, in turn, can affect our bodies by disrupting our endocrine system, possibly causing hormone-dependent cancers (such as breast, ovarian, and prostate cancer), and serving as a major contributor to the global emergence of antibiotic-resistant organisms like methicillin-resistant *Staphylococcus aureus* (MRSA).

The next step would be to minimize your consumption of pork because so much of the supply is not grass-fed, free-range, and organic.

AVOCADOS

Avocados boast many health benefits thanks to their star nutrients: mono- and poly-unsaturated fats, phytosterols, alpha-linolenic acid (think omega-3 fatty acids), and carotenoids. Research has shown that avocados reduce inflammation, blood sugar elevation, and cholesterol and lessen the effects of osteoarthritis and rheumatoid arthritis. The avocado's nutritious oils and fats also help moisturize hair and tone skin. Avocado is a wonderful replacement for other oils and fats in cooking; use it when you would typically spread on butter or mayonnaise. Four ounces of avocado has 227 calories, 9 grams fiber, 3 grams protein, and 21 grams fat, of which 75 percent are healthful mono- and polyunsaturated fats. Examples of carotenoids in avocado include alpha- and beta-carotene, zeaxanthin, lutein, neochrome, neoxanthin, and chrysanthemaxanthin. Many of these compounds also slow the progression of vision problems, such as macular degeneration. Thanks to the high fat content in avocado, if you add avocado to a salad, you'll increase the absorption of antioxidant carotenoids in the salad by 200 to 400 percent.

BRASSICAS, CRUCIFEROUS VEGETABLES, AND LEAFY GREENS

Cruciferous vegetables include arugula, bok choy, broccoli, Brussels sprouts, cabbage, cauliflower, Chinese cabbage, collard greens, daikon radish, horseradish, kale, kohlrabi, mustard greens, rutabaga, turnip, and watercress. As a group, these vegetables are super-foods known for containing a high content of antioxidants like vitamin C and manganese. They are also a great source of protein and fiber. These vegetables contain sulforaphanes, which offset inflammation by enhancing phase two detoxification in the liver. For example, broccoli provides two-thirds of the protein you get from a chicken breast and 9 grams fiber. If you are looking for the perfect cancer-fighting food, cruciferous vegetables are the choice. Multiple studies have found that a special class of compounds in these vegetables, called glucosinolates, have potent anticancer properties.

Due to its recent popularity, kale deserves special mention, separate from other cruciferous vegetables and leafy greens. Chefs praise kale because it's easy to grow and use in the kitchen. Many grocery stores have shelves lined with kale products, from chips to premade salads. Given this spotlight, you may be surprised to learn that kale contains high quantities of oxalic acid, which can build up in the body and cause kidney stones and interfere with calcium absorption. (Interesting fact: The plant does this to protect itself from predators.) Lightly steam kale for about 5 minutes instead of eating it raw, because steaming inactivates the oxalic acid and boosts the immense nutrient benefits, including its cholesterol-lowering properties. To ensure even cooking and easier chewing, cut the leaves and stems into ¼- to ½-in [6- to 12-mm] slices.

Kale's cancer-prevention effects are derived from its high concentration of carotenoids and flavonoids, powerful antioxidants, as well as from its high concentration of isothiocyanates, shown to dramatically improve both phase 1 and phase 2 of the liver's detoxification pathway, resulting in a huge surge in the body's detoxification capacity.

CITRUS FRUITS

Any way you squeeze it, citrus fruits, especially clementines, grapefruits, lemons, limes, and oranges, are health heroes. We usually praise them for their high vitamin C content during the cold season, but there's so much more to love about citrus. Due to their high water content, any type of citrus will provide hydration and electrolytes to thirsty bodies. Citrus flavonoids have also been shown to neutralize free radicals, potentially preventing the growth of cancer cells. Their inflammation-fighting properties are found in the skin as well as the juice and flesh.

DARK CHOCOLATE

Dark chocolate (70 percent cocoa or more) may be the first guilt-free dessert prescribed by doctors. Research has shown that it's good for the heart, pancreas, and gastrointestinal system (ground zero for inflammation). It improves the body's response to a carbohydrate sugar–enriched meal by improving insulin sensitivity, thereby potentially delaying or preventing the onset of prediabetes and diabetes if consumed regularly in small quantities. The fibrous cacao particles that go undigested boost the healthy bacteria in your gut. Studies have also shown that 1 oz [30 g] of dark chocolate with 70 percent or greater cacao content improves cardiovascular function in healthy people and in cardiovascular patients by enhancing arterial blood flow and modestly lowering blood pressure.

DRIED CHILES

Chiles are classified as nightshades, which can be problematic for people suffering from inflammation-related conditions. If you are not bothered by nightshades or, more specifically, by chiles, then chiles may be quite beneficial for you. The heat you experience when eating dried chiles, such as ancho, chipotle, and guajillo, relates to the capsaicin content. Capsaicin is a well-known powerful pain reliever and anti-inflammatory agent and reduces the risk of developing diabetes when consumed regularly. Capsaicin lowers a neuropeptide called substance P, which may reduce nerve and joint pain. The research is convincing enough that companies sell capsaicin lotions and patches for the treatment of joint pain, such as osteoarthritis, and neuropathic pain resulting from diabetes and sciatica. (The application of capsaicin is painful at first, so people experience discomfort for a while before they experience relief.) In addition, research has shown that people who eat dried chiles increase their metabolic rate for 30 minutes, require less insulin in response to a carbohydrate-rich meal, and prevent oxidation (free radical production) of triglycerides and cholesterol. Capsaicin concentrates in the flesh and seeds of the pepper, so if you can handle the heat, always use the seeds when cooking them. The hotter the pepper, the greater the capsaicin content.

DRIED SPICES

Spicing food for both taste and dietary benefits is nothing new. Confucius was a proponent of consuming ginger, in fresh and dried and ground form, with every meal for digestive benefits. Today, we most often think of spice as simply a flavor agent, but it also does the body good, adds complexity to dishes, and takes the place of excessive use of salt or sugar. Cinnamon has been shown to reduce bloat and discomfort-inducing bacteria in the digestive tract, increase overall circulation, and regulate sugar levels after a meal. Turmeric is a proven anti-inflammatory and anticancer agent, making it a great addition to foods for those with arthritis or living with cancer. You can find it in capsule form at the health-food store, but sprinkling it into savory dishes is my favorite way of increasing my turmeric intake. Like many other spices, black pepper acts as a thermogenic, increasing your metabolic rate and increasing the absorption of turmeric and many other compounds that have poor bioavailability (the natural ability to be absorbed by the body) by 2,000 percent.

EGGS

Many doctors call eggs the "perfect food," given their high content of protein, vitamins A and B, and biotin. Eggs help offset inflammation because they contain the potent carotenoids zeaxanthin and lutein (both good for vision), as well as choline (good for brain and heart function). The first rule for enjoying these oval powerhouses is to *always* buy organic. Organic eggs not only have higher levels of omega-3 fatty acids, but they lack residues of the antibiotics Tylenol, Benadryl, and arsenic that are added to the feed of conventionally raised chickens and may be present in low levels in the meat. (Yes, arsenic! Conventional producers often add it to the feed mix to prevent infections.) The second rule is to not get tricked by clever marketing strategies; "pasture raised" and "cage free" are *not* interchangeable! While your best bet is always to buy from local farmers who take pride in raising free-roaming hens, pasture raised is the next best thing. Simply put, true pasture-raised hens live in open fields and are allowed to forage independently for their food. "Cage-free" or even "free-range" hens are often just moved around from cage to cage or are merely given moments outside. Loopholes in the regulations still allow the use of such health-halo labels.

FISH:
SALMON AND OTHER OILY TYPES

Adults, especially pregnant women, and children should eat three servings of cold-water fish weekly. Cold-water fish, such as salmon, rainbow trout, black cod (sable fish), whitefish, Atlantic herring, Atlantic mackerel, anchovies, and Pacific sardines contain low levels of mercury and high amounts of polyunsaturated fatty acids. These omega-3 fatty acids have been shown to reduce inflammation and improve heart health, autoimmune conditions, and mood disorders, as well as promote skin and nail health. They are truly a wonder food. Countless patients have seen their pain-related conditions improve while on a steady diet of cold-water fish. To limit mercury exposure, avoid eating fish that live at the top of the food chain, such as shark, swordfish, tilefish, and king mackerel.

GARLIC AND ONIONS

These and other short-chain fructo-oligosaccharides (scFOS) are delicious sources of sweet low-calorie carbohydrates. Since these foods aren't fully digested in the gut, the remaining material feeds the healthy bacteria living in our intestines, resulting in a healthier gut. Through this process, these foods also boost the immune system and lower inflammation. The scFOS provide almost half the sweetness of table sugar without all the calories. In addition to onions and garlic, other foods that contains scFOS are leeks, asparagus, Jerusalem artichokes, jicama roots, chicory, burdock roots, and dandelion roots.

Notoriously called the stinking rose, garlic is a member of the allium family, which includes leeks and onions. Many of its health benefits are derived from sulfur compounds (allicin, alliin, 1, 2-vinyldithin, hydrogen sulfide), and include reduced inflammation and oxidation, as well as modestly lowering oxidized cholesterol, triglycerides, blood pressure, and reducing blood clotting. Garlic may even be protective against cancer. It's also a source of manganese, selenium, and vitamin B_6. To obtain maximal health benefits, purchase garlic fresh (rather than using flakes or powder), chop it, and let it sit for 10 to 15 minutes to let the alliinase enzymes activate before using it in a recipe. Although garlic is ideally consumed in its raw form, many find it difficult to tolerate; if that is the case for you, add the garlic toward the latter part of the cooking process, which lessens its digestive impact.

GREEN TEA

Green tea leaves are unfermented and therefore contain higher amounts of polyphenols than oolong or black tea. Polyphenols are powerful antioxidants, the best known being epigallocatechin gallate. Green tea also contains alkaloids such as caffeine, theophylline (used to treat asthma), and theobromine (used in toothpaste for its antimicrobial benefits), which provides the tea's energy-boosting effect. L-theanine, an amino acid present in the tea, has been shown to improve mental clarity and quiet nerves. The health benefits of green tea are well known to traditional healing practices; used as an everyday medicine, it improves heart health, removes excess fluid from the body, regulates blood sugar, improves digestion, and calms the mind. Recent studies have shown that drinking 3 cups daily is associated with reducing the risk of cancer, heart disease, and stroke by 20 to 30 percent. As if that weren't enough, studies suggest that green tea may also increase metabolism and prompt the body to preferentially burn fat cells, helping with weight loss.

HERBS

Since antiquity, herbs have been prized because they not only add a flavorful dimension to a variety of recipes but are also superfoods. As a leafy herb, oregano demonstrates terrific antioxidant benefits. Oregano oil has been used as a natural antibiotic. Adding rosemary or lavender to a dish can calm anxiety, relieve pain, and improve mood. Parsley deserves credit as more than garnish; its volatile oils have been shown to disrupt the growth of cancer cells in animal studies. Moroccans provide a good example for the rest of us by enjoying the anti-inflammatory properties of tea made from an infusion of mint to aid digestion and cleanse the palate.

LEGUMES

Legumes include beans, peas, and lentils. There is a huge variety to choose from: black, navy, kidney, garbanzo (think hummus), and soy (think tofu and tempeh). All are excellent sources of fiber, protein, iron, calcium, zinc, and B vitamins and help minimize inflammation by phytochemicals. Just one serving of cooked black beans (1 cup [170 g]) offers 15 grams fiber (more than the typical American gets in an entire day) and protein. Just ½ cup [125 g] of cooked lentils offers 30 grams fiber and 25 grams protein, making them an excellent choice for vegetarians or those looking to lessen their meat consumption. Garbanzo beans are a great pick for those looking to increase the consumption of folate and manganese. Just 1 cup [250 g] of cooked garbanzos has 14 grams each fiber and protein.

Despite significant debate in the news about the risks and benefits of soy, the science shows that soy is an excellent food source. It comes in many forms: soymilk, soybeans (edamame), tofu, tempeh, miso, soy "meat," and soy "cheese." These forms are preferable over the more concentrated and processed soy protein often found in energy bars and powders. Soy is low in saturated fat and is a great source of fiber, polyunsaturated fat, protein, vitamins, and minerals.

MUSHROOMS

Mushrooms provide astonishing health-promoting benefits. These wonder foods come in a dizzying array of edible varieties. Because they grow in moist soil, they absorb components both good and bad, so it's best to buy organic. In addition to containing vitamins and minerals, mushrooms make a hearty and heart-healthy substitute for meat. You can find mushroom supplements for many different health purposes, but eating them is the best place to start. My favorites include cremini, shiitake, reishi "spirit plant," turkey tail "cloud," and white button. All are beneficial to the immune system and have anti-inflammatory effects.

NATURAL SWEETENERS

Which type of sweetener is best? All natural sweeteners have one thing in common—ultimately they are nothing more than sugars that you add to your food, and, as such, should be used in limited quantities. With the exception of honey, the differences between sweeteners such as maple syrup, agave, cane sugar, and white sugar are minimal. Therefore, base your preference on taste over nutrient quality, look for organic versions to limit the consumption of pesticides in addition to sugar, and try to use the least amount possible to sweeten treats.

Agave, which comes from the blue agave plant (the same source for tequila), tastes sweeter than beet or cane sugar but has a lower glycemic index (the measure of how a carbohydrate-containing food increases glucose in the blood). Does this sound too good to be true? Unfortunately, it is. The reason that agave has less sugar yet tastes so sweet is that it contains highly processed fructose (think high-fructose corn syrup), which is very hard for the liver to process and ultimately can lead to fatty liver and promote obesity. Consumption of fructose is a major contributor to the rising epidemic of fatty liver in the Western world. Agave contains 60 calories per 1 Tbsp compared to 40 calories for white sugar.

Of the natural sweeteners, honey seems to have the most health benefits, showing promise in healing skin wounds, reducing cough and diarrhea in children (give only to children age 2 and older), and lessening the effects of environmental allergies, to name a few.

Maple syrup can contain more than 54 antioxidants (more than double that of refined sugars), but you would have to consume huge quantities to reap all the potential benefits. The nutrient contribution would be negligible compared with the damage to your body caused by all those added sugars. When it comes to adding a sweetener to food, honey and maple syrup are your best choices.

OILS

Olive oil is a rich source of polyphenols, which provide both anti-inflammatory and antioxidant benefits. Try to use extra-virgin olive oil (from the first pressing) for most of your cooking. More than 70 percent of its fat content comes from a monounsaturated fat called oleic acid, which has been found to help lower blood pressure, reduce LDL (bad) cholesterol, and increase HDL (good) cholesterol, among other heart-healthy properties. The closest contender is canola oil, with 60 percent of its fat derived from monounsaturated fat.

Coconut oil earned a bad reputation in the 1980s when it was highly processed and contained partially hydrogenated oil, among other unhealthful additives. The fresh-pressed coconut oil available in whole form today (that is, not in processed foods) is a healthful option (albeit less so than olive oil or canola oil). Although 90 percent of the fat in coconut oil is saturated—compared with butter at 64 percent—virgin and refined coconut oil, unlike butter, contains saturated fat as a medium-chain triglyceride, called lauric acid. Lauric acid has been shown to be an easily digestible source of sustained energy for the elderly and for athletes and to increase HDL cholesterol levels.

QUINOA

Quinoa, which can be treated like a grain but is the seed of the plant and an ideal gluten-free food, has been a staple in South America for five thousand years. It was considered an optimal food for astronauts because it has a high protein-to-carbohydrate ratio, is a complete protein (it doesn't need to combine with another compound to deliver protein to the body), is high in healthful fats and fiber, and is a complex carbohydrate. As a result, it has many of the beneficial macro- and micronutrients you look for in a food. It has anti-inflammatory and antioxidant effects, improves the regulation of sugar in the bloodstream, lowers LDL cholesterol, and serves as a short-term and long-term fuel source. Remember to rinse quinoa well before cooking to remove the saponins, which are a naturally occurring pesticide and give the quinoa a bitter taste.

SEEDS

Sunflower, sesame, pumpkin, and other seeds are excellent sources of healthful fats, fiber, and protein. They also provide manganese, magnesium (helps lessen PMS, blood pressure), vitamin B_6 (promotes nerve function and heart health), potassium (lowers blood pressure), the full spectrum of vitamin E (supports heart health and offsets cancer risk), zinc (promotes immune system and prostate health), plant-based omega-3 fatty acids (improves heart and skin health and treats autoimmune conditions), plant sterols (lowers cholesterol and promotes prostate health), and other vital nutrients. Research has shown that eating a small handful of seeds most days of the week can help lower blood sugar levels, improve cholesterol, reduce heart attack risk, improve digestion, and decrease cancer risk.

SWEET POTATOES

Not all spuds are created equal. Sweet potatoes are far more nutritious than their pale counterpart, the white potato in all its varieties. Our taste buds don't lie. There is a reason that caramelized sweet potatoes taste so yummy—they effectively become candy! To get the greatest health benefits from sweet potatoes and manage their sugar load, cook them just long enough so that they soften but not until they become mushy. Once a sweet potato has caramelized (and become mushy), the fiber has broken down, enabling the potato to be digested rapidly, in the same way a simple starch is processed by the body.

Russet potatoes, like white bread and pasta, are a simple starch or carbohydrate and are best consumed in moderation. As you digest them, they break down quickly into sugar, whereas sweet potatoes, a complex starch or carbohydrate, take longer to digest. As a result, the sugar takes longer to enter the body, causing a slower rise in blood sugar, which leads to a less dramatic increase in insulin levels. Over the long term, simple starches are much more likely to cause insulin resistance and diabetes than complex starches.

Consume the skins of any type of potato whenever possible to reap the best vitamin and mineral reward.

TREE NUTS

Raw or toasted almonds, cashews, chestnuts, hazelnuts, pecans, pistachios, and walnuts are rich sources of healthful fats, fiber, protein, and antioxidants. Nuts enjoyed as a snack several times a week provides sustained energy. Eating a small handful of nuts or 1 Tbsp nut butter four days a week as part of a Mediterranean diet has been shown to lower blood sugar levels after eating a carbohydrate-heavy meal, reduce LDL cholesterol, and lower the risk of heart disease by 30 percent. Nuts also deliver a boost of sustained energy while making you feel full and satisfied. Chestnuts, pecans, and walnuts (a good source of omega-3 fatty acids) provide the highest antioxidant content of all tree nuts.

— foods to avoid —

I am constantly hearing from colleagues and friends about how they can no longer tolerate gluten or dairy or corn, and most don't know why they've developed these intolerances. Let me break it down for you very simply in the following entries. I tend to be hypersensitive to most of these foods, so I use very few of them in my recipes. (Some you won't see at all.) Even if you seem to tolerate these foods well, some of you may notice you feel better when you remove some or all of them from your diet. My goal? To make food that tastes so good you don't miss these foods at all.

ALCOHOL

If you are looking to curb inflammation, it's important to determine how much alcohol is tolerable and what types are the best options. Alcohol in modest amounts raises the good (HDL) cholesterol, improves insulin sensitivity, and reduces blood clotting. Research has shown that adults who drink modest quantities of alcohol most days of the week are 25 to 40 percent less likely to develop heart disease and experience strokes compared to people who drink too much or none at all.

How much is enough? Studies suggest that women should drink one serving and men one to two servings most days of the week. A serving equals 5 oz [150 ml] wine, 12 oz [360 ml] beer, and 1½ oz [45 ml] hard liquor. Women should drink less than men because higher quantities deplete folic acid, which in turn causes many problems, including increasing the risk for breast cancer by as much as 40 percent.

Alcohol can be problematic for certain populations. For example, most East Asians have a genetic variant that produces more acetaldehyde after consuming alcohol than seen in other populations. Acetaldehyde is toxic and causes nausea, headache, and skin flushing. People with this reaction are also six to ten times more likely to develop esophageal cancer if they drink. If you are gluten-intolerant, you want to drink gluten-free beer, since many beers are made from grains, such as wheat, barley, or rye that contain gluten proteins. Interestingly, the distillation process required to make hard liquor removes gluten; consequently, gluten-sensitive people frequently are able to drink rye whiskey, for example. However, there have been reports of people with celiac disease having bad reactions to hard liquor as well.

If you get headaches after drinking red wine, it's likely due to the tannin content. Tannins cause the astringent taste (that dry, puckering effect) in certain wines. A recent study showed that people who consumed red wines with lower tannin content had fewer headaches than those who drank higher tannin content wines. Do your research and find those lower-tannin wines. South American Cabernet Sauvignon and Merlot have fewer tannins than Malbec from the same region and also much fewer tannins than their French equivalents, for example.

As part of an anti-inflammatory diet, it's important to limit your intake of sugar and refined carbohydrates, and your choice of alcohol is no exception. Liquor is highly distilled and therefore is void of sugar; of course, the sugar content of what you may add to the drink could vary considerably. "Light" and pilsner beers and dry wines have a lower sugar and carbohydrate content than their counterparts.

COFFEE

The antioxidant effects of coffee are well known, and drinking to 2 to 3 cups (12 to 18 oz [320 to 530 ml]) daily improves cardiovascular health, with more being harmful to your health. For many people, the tannins in coffee cause stomach upset by irritating the stomach lining and can worsen gastroesophogeal reflux. If your blood pressure is too high, consider eliminating coffee. Caffeinated coffees increase the sympathetic nervous system's "fight or flight" stress response, which may increase anxiety, irritability, and agitation, and negatively affect sleep quality.

CORN

Corn has been the second biggest problem food in my diet. When I realized I was gluten intolerant, I started to replace flour with corn in tortillas and wraps and even in some pastas. But I still suffered from bouts of stomach pain when eating a lot of corn.

What I experienced is a classic example of immune-response cross-reactivity. I had developed antibodies to certain gluten proteins, and these antibodies may react with different proteins in other food groups, including corn. When I eat corn, my immune system sees it as a foreign invader and unleashes antibodies to fight off the invasion, resulting in body aches and an assortment of other reactions. I discovered that embarking on a full elimination diet can be very helpful. When I added corn back into my diet, I noticed that my symptoms worsened, thereby confirming corn is a trigger food for me.

Even if you enjoy corn and your immune system does not react to it, be mindful that genetically modified sweet corn entered the United States in 2012. Corn is sprayed heavily with pesticides during production, so this is one food for which organic really is better for you. To avoid eating GMO corn and exposing yourself to harmful pesticide and herbicides, always purchase certified organic corn. The Non-GMO Project, an organization focused on education and preservation of non-GMO foods, provides more useful information on this topic.

DAIRY

The two main types of dairy intolerance are lactose intolerance and casein sensitivity. Lactose intolerance is the inability to digest the lactose sugar in dairy products. This digestive problem affects 50 to 80 percent of African Americans, Latinos, and Asians and about 20 percent of Caucasians. Typical symptoms include significant gas, abdominal bloating and pain, and diarrhea within hours after ingesting dairy. Milk and ice cream have the greatest concentration of lactose and therefore cause the greatest symptoms. While yogurt has similar concentrations, the live cultures seem to make it a more tolerable dairy product for people with this condition.

Casein sensitivity is similar to gluten sensitivity in that the body has developed antibodies to the food's major protein component, in this case casein. Consequently, people with casein sensitivity experience gastrointestinal and extra-gastrointestinal symptoms in similar fashion as people suffering from gluten sensitivity. There is significant overlap between people with gluten sensitivity and those with casein sensitivity. Many healing systems uphold the belief that dairy products, with the possible exception of yogurt, create mucus and congestion in the body. If you suffer from chronic sinusitis, environmental allergies, headaches, and chronic mucus production, you may want to experiment with eliminating dairy for four weeks and observe your symptoms.

If you find that eliminating dairy improves your health, it's important to find other sources of calcium. Recent research has shown that adults need 700 mg calcium daily, but that higher doses are associated with increased risk of heart attack and no reduction in osteoporosis or hip fractures. Excellent nondairy sources of calcium include broccoli rabe, collard greens, bok choy, soy beans, and canned sardines and salmon (with bones). Fortified sources include almond and rice milk, orange juice, and tofu.

FOOD COLORING

Artificial food coloring has been clearly associated with behavior changes in children, including hyperactivity, aggression, agitation, and irritability. Our daily consumption of artificial food coloring, as measured by the quantity of dye certified by the United States Food and Drug Administration for use in consumables, has increased fivefold since the 1950s. Examples of these additives include FD&C Green No. 3, Red No. 3 and 40, and Blue No. 1 and 2. While we know that the ingredients in artificial food coloring are not good for you, no one has ever quantified exactly how much we are consuming. Studies in the 1970s assumed children were consuming 20 to 30 mg daily of artificial coloring and used this assumption in evaluating the safety of food coloring. A 2014 Purdue University study calculated the exact amounts in various consumer products and found that children are consuming much higher doses of artificial coloring than previously estimated. Typical cereals, beverages, and sweets containing these artificial additives frequently had 35 mg in one serving. As you might imagine, children could easily exceed a 100-mg daily dose, which is more than three times the dose previously studied. If you want to use food coloring, look for natural food colorings made from beets, turmeric, elderberry, paprika, saffron, and butterfly pea.

GLUTEN

If you are one of 24 million Americans with celiac disease or nonceliac gluten sensitivity, you should avoid grains containing gluten, such as wheat, barley, rye, and sometimes oats.

People with celiac disease have what is called an adaptive immune response that is specific to one or more of the gluten proteins. This occurs when antibodies come in contact with gluten proteins, which causes a robust inflammatory reaction resulting in disruption of the intestinal lining (known as "leaky gut"). Gluten and other proteins, as well as toxins and bacteria, are then allowed to cross the gut-blood barrier, causing inflammation and extra-gastrointestinal symptoms, such as fatigue, joint aches, and headaches. Celiac disease has genetic determinants and familial inheritance and is identified via specific diagnostic testing.

Nonceliac gluten sensitivity is not well understood. It is considered a less-severe reaction than celiac disease. People typically have a nonspecific immune response, and therefore some may not generate gluten-specific antibodies. Typically these individuals experience less inflammation of the gut lining after eating these foods. That said, these people tend to have similar symptoms as those with celiac disease, namely bloating, gas, and pain, as well as extra-gastrointestinal symptoms.

Wheat allergy can be diagnosed using skin-prick tests, wheat Ig-E blood tests, and a food challenge. If you have symptoms concerning for gluten-related disorder, try an elimination diet for four weeks combined with journaling your symptoms. If you feel better, get tested for wheat allergy and celiac disease. If both tests are negative, you likely have nonceliac gluten sensitivity or you may have something called FODMAPs. FODMAPs was identified by Dr. Sue Shepard in the late 1990s. The acronym stands for "fermentable oligo-, di-, mono-saccharides and polyos." People with this condition have difficulty absorbing this collection of short-chain carbohydrates and therefore doctors advise them to avoid foods that contain lactose, fructose, fructans, sugar alcohols, and galactans, such as ice cream, ricotta cheese, cashews, lentils, miso, gluten, apples, blackberries, artichokes, and cauliflower. Within one to two weeks of eliminating these foods, sufferers report feeling remarkably better.

Many grains and healthful natural flours can be used to replace traditional wheat flour in cooking and baking. Just as with using refined wheat flours, the key is to use moderation. When I want to replicate gluten, here's where I turn: For wheat-flour alternatives, I use rice flour, chickpea flour, almond flour, buckwheat, and blends of all of these. For wheat-flour substitutes for baking, I use one of the flours that have been created to act as similarly to white flour as possible, such as Cup4Cup or Bob's Red Mill Gluten-Free Flour Mix.

NIGHTSHADES

Nightshades are a family of flowering plants, easily identifiable by the green elfish "hats" that connect the fruits and vegetables to their stems. The most common nightshades we consume are eggplants, bell peppers, potatoes, chiles, and tomatoes. Many nightshades have powerful health properties, such as the vitamins A and C found in tomatoes, along with many antioxidants. However, nightshades all contain glycoalkaloids, natural pesticides that can cause joint pain and other arthritic symptoms (and potentially contribute to leaky gut.) Bottom line? If you're not sensitive to nightshades, eggplants, peppers, potatoes, and tomatoes can be wonderful additions to your diet. In this book, I've listed alternative ingredients when necessary in case you are indeed sensitive.

SALT

Have you ever noticed that what one person finds overly salted, another finds not salted enough? Your perception of saltiness depends on the amount of salt you have been eating in the recent past. If you reduce your salt intake, you won't notice the difference in the saltiness of your food after seven days because your taste buds adjust rapidly. Too much salt causes health problems, including high blood pressure and kidney disease. People should eat less than 2,400 mg sodium daily (1 tsp table salt), and ideally less than 1,500 mg per day if they are older than 50 or have high blood pressure. Salt is about 40 percent sodium by weight, so 1,500 mg sodium equals about 4,000 mg salt per day. The best ways to avoid salt are to prepare your own meals, accentuate spices, and avoid canned, processed, and fast foods.

SUGAR

We all know sugar isn't good for us, especially in its refined state with its potential pesticide load. That said, we live in the real world where sugar exists in everything, so try to use it in extreme moderation. (The only times I use refined sugar these days is to make a classic dessert for special occasions.)

Sugar is the number-one food additive in our food supply. Added sugar is everywhere and often hidden. You can find it in spaghetti sauce, hot dogs, crackers, cereals, pizza, peanut butter, canned rice, yogurt, luncheon meats, and more. If you read food labels, added sugars appear as "brown sugar," "corn sweetener," "corn syrup," "fruit juice concentrates," "high-fructose corn syrup," "honey," "invert sugar," "malt sugar," "molasses," "raw sugar," "sugar," "syrup," and "simple syrup." Also look for words ending in "ose," such as *dextrose, glucose, lactose, sucrose,* and *maltose.*

Studies have documented that sugar floods the pleasure center of our brain, called the nucleus accumbens, with dopamine, in similar fashion to sex and drugs of addiction. With the introduction of low-fat foods in the 1980s, manufacturers replaced calories derived from fat with added sugar. Between 1950 and 2000, average sugar consumption increased 40 percent from 110 to 152 lb [50 to 69 kg] per year, primarily with the introduction of high-fructose corn syrup into the marketplace. This translates into consuming 32 tsp [160 g] sugar daily; it's no surprise then that rates of prediabetes and diabetes in teenagers have soared from 9 percent to 23 percent between 2000 and 2008. Current recommendations are to limit sugar consumption to 10 tsp [40 g] daily, which is equivalent to drinking a 12-oz [260-ml] soft drink. The effect of these added sugars is dramatic. For example, drinking one can of soda daily increases a child's risk for becoming obese by 60 percent and increases an adult's risk for becoming a type 2 diabetic by 80 percent.

Keep in mind that refined carbohydrates such as white flour are quickly converted into sugar molecules in the body and are therefore equivalent to eating sugar in its raw form. Calories from either added sugar or refined carbohydrates have profoundly negative effects on the body and leave you craving sweet foods within a few hours after eating. Calories from fat and protein, on the other hand, leave you feeling satisfied and full longer, without the sugar cravings.

SUGAR SUBSTITUTES

There has been limited research examining the risks and benefits of using sugar substitutes such as sucralose (Splenda), aspartame (Equal), and saccharin (Sweet'N Low). However, a recent paper published in the science research journal *Nature* found that sugar substitutes can profoundly disrupt our body's ability to handle sugar, even when compared with consuming sugar itself. The researchers demonstrated that these noncaloric artificial sweeteners (NAS) alter the bacteria living in the gastrointestinal tract in a manner that changes how the body handles glucose (sugar), resulting in a condition called glucose intolerance (also known as insulin resistance), a condition that causes diabetes.

Based on this latest research, it follows that we should avoid NAS altogether. If you are determined to enhance sweetness, use limited quantities of added sugar instead.

— the food-first pantry —

In addition to keeping all the feel-good foods in my house, I try to have on hand basic pantry and perishable staples. They provide a basis for cooking well with speed and diversity when I'm short on time (which is all the time).

apples	fish
avocados	flours
beans	frozen berries and mangoes
beef, grass-fed	frozen vegetables
broccoli	garlic
carrots	ginger
cauliflower	gluten-free pasta
celery	goat cheese
chicken and/or vegetable stock	greek yogurt
chicken, free-range and organic	green tea
citrus	herbs
cornmeal	honey
curry paste	kale
dark chocolate (70 percent cacao or more)	lettuces
	light agave nectar
dijon mustard	maple syrup, grade B
dried chiles	mayonnaise (organic canola oil–based) or Vegenaise
eggs	

milk	salt
mushrooms	seeds
nuts and nut milks	shallots
oats	spices
oils	sprouts
onions, yellow and red	sugar
organic popcorn kernels	sweet potatoes
parmesan cheese	tamari, low-sodium and gluten-free
peanut butter	tofu
polenta	vanilla beans
quinoa	vinegars
rice	

— before you start cooking —

Everything in this book is gluten-free. Many recipes are vegetarian and vegan or can easily be made so. Fewer than a dozen recipes use dairy. When eaten collectively, these recipes are cleansing, restorative, and energizing.

Before I set out to cook a recipe, I always want to know how long will it take, so I've indicated that throughout. I never want to be in the middle of a recipe and then figure out it's going to take me three hours when I initially thought it would take me only thirty minutes. I'm sure you feel the same.

After commuting home from work, I cook dinner most nights. I'm known at work for my adherence to a weekly schedule that involves meal planning, budgeting, and strategic trips to the grocery store. Boring? Maybe, but I can't tell you how much my cooking has improved and how much creativity has been recouped by knowing that everything I need to make dinner is already in the house when I arrive home after a long day. When I decided I wanted to improve what I ate, meal planning ensured I had the right ingredients to make the new recipes I had developed, preventing me from falling back into the familiar cooking that triggered inflammation. It also kept me to a budget. Embracing the planning piece of cooking is the secret to improving the way we eat.

— meal planning —

Once a week, I sit down and make a plan. I create a handwritten chart with each day, Monday through Sunday, at the top, and I label *breakfast*, *lunch*, *dinner*, and *snacks* down the side. Then I plot my plan for the week. I start by filling in any meals where we'll be out or are having people in, then if any of those meals produce good leftovers, I'll write those in for lunch the next day. I try to vary my dinners in cost, types of protein, and family requests to keep meals interesting. If I know I'm making a homemade snack or two that week, I'll fill it in under snacks a few times and maybe breakfast. (Granola is a good example. I might use it with yogurt in the morning and package it up as a snack, too.)

This fifteen-minute exercise is like a jigsaw puzzle. The more you do it, the quicker you get. The creativity comes when you realize that once all of the ingredients are in the house, you can cook whatever, whenever that week. The exception to this is fresh fish or beef. I cook fish the day I buy it, and I usually cook beef or poultry within two days.

budgeting

People think I'm crazy when I tell them I can buy a week's worth of food for my family of four at a high-quality market for what many couples spend per week. Plus I buy about 75 percent organic foods. How do I do it? I've committed to learning what key items typically cost in the grocery store. (For me, that list to memorize includes wild salmon, organic free-range eggs, and organic in-season apples, for example.) By paying attention once or twice when you go to the store, you'll see how easy it is to remember the cost of your favorite items. Focus on the staples you buy the most and try to memorize a few more each visit to the market. Figuring this out allows you to budget directly on your shopping list, giving you an idea of what you'll spend before you even walk into the store. The checkers at my grocery store love watching me accurately predict what I'm going to spend. Soon, you'll be doing the same.

shopping list

Making a list will save you so much time and money. Since I started making mine, I've stopped having to throw out a bunch of unused ingredients at the end of each week. Begin by listing all of the ingredients you need for the recipes you've chosen. Then cross out anything you already have in your pantry, refrigerator, or freezer. (Once you've had some practice, you'll probably have an idea of what you already have.) Fill in any miscellaneous items you might need, such as dish soap and toothpaste. Now if you're serious about budgeting, approximate how much each item will cost you and total everything. If it looks like you'll be spending a lot more than you'd like, go back and look at the recipes you've chosen, remembering that beans, grains, and veggie-centric dishes are a lot less expensive than meat-based ones. Sometimes I'll drop in one or two recipes for favorites like Black Bean Soup or Curried Lentils with Basmati Rice, and I'm right back on track.

My goal is to go to the market once a week for the bulk of the shopping and go back a second time toward the end of the week to get highly perishable foods, such as fish and stone fruits. Once I'm home, I unload it all and try to prep just two or three simple recipes in order to get off on the right start for the week.

That's all there is to it. You'll see this is a key tactic to cooking and feeling better.

chapter

1

BASICS AND MAKE-AHEAD RECIPES

Because I work full-time, commute, and have a family, people are constantly asking if I *really* cook most nights. Yes! And I don't have a team of helpers, either. It's just my husband and me figuring out the shopping and cooking. Having foundational basics like vinaigrettes, chimichurri sauce, romesco, cooked quinoa, and almond milk at the ready is key to producing healthful meals quickly during the week. Adding these to your repertoire instead of reaching for packaged products will help you cut sugar, sodium, and refined ingredients from your weekly diet.

FRENCH VINAIGRETTE

I studied French in Aix-en-Provence for a blissful semester twenty years ago. Every time I had a great salad when I was there, I'd ask what was in the vinaigrette. Nine times out of ten, I got the same response—it was this recipe. You can substitute organic canola, walnut, or even grapeseed oil for the extra-virgin olive oil and practically any vinegar for the sherry vinegar, but for the combination that pairs with the most salads, this one is still my go-to.

PREPARATION TIME
10 minutes

MAKES
3/4 cup / 180 ml

2 Tbsp Dijon mustard

2 tsp minced shallot

¼ cup [60 ml] sherry vinegar

Kosher salt

Freshly ground black pepper

½ cup [120 ml] extra-virgin olive oil

Place the Dijon mustard and shallot in a small bowl. Whisk in the vinegar. Add a generous pinch of salt and a fresh grinding of pepper. Allow the shallots to sit in the vinegar for about 5 minutes. Slowly whisk in the olive oil to create an emulsified vinaigrette. Taste (I like to dip a piece of lettuce into the vinaigrette to taste), adding more salt and pepper if desired.

Store in an airtight glass container in the refrigerator for up to 1 week. Whisk again just before serving to re-emulsify.

CURRIED BLACK PEPPER VINAIGRETTE

Curry spice blends (that contain turmeric) are a wonderful, unexpected addition to a basic vinaigrette and are another way to incorporate more turmeric in your diet. This vinaigrette becomes the perfect dressing for grain salads and lettuces, and is also delicious tossed with roasted chicken or as a glaze for shrimp.

PREPARATION TIME
10 minutes

MAKES
3/4 cup / 180 ml

¼ cup [60 ml] lime juice

2 tsp honey

2 tsp curry powder, plus more as needed

½ tsp freshly ground black pepper

¼ tsp cayenne pepper

½ cup [120 ml] organic canola oil

Kosher salt

Place the lime juice, honey, curry powder, black pepper, and cayenne in a small bowl. Whisk until smooth. Slowly whisk in the canola oil until combined. Season with salt. Taste (I like to dip a piece of lettuce into the vinaigrette to taste), adding more salt or spice if desired.

Store in an airtight glass container in the refrigerator for up to 1 week. Whisk again just before serving to re-emulsify.

GARLIC-LEMON VINAIGRETTE

Hands down, this is the most popular vinaigrette in my house. I use it to coax kale into a delicious salad; toss it with quinoa or other grains to bind grain salads; and pour it on practically every chopped salad I make. If you love the taste of Caesar salad, simply add 2 to 3 Tbsp of grated Parmigiano-Reggiano to some chopped romaine with this vinaigrette (pictured opposite, in the bottle), and you're in business.

PREPARATION TIME
10 minutes

MAKES
3/4 cups / 180 ml

1 garlic clove

Kosher salt

1 Tbsp plus 1 tsp Dijon mustard, plus more as needed

1/4 cup [60 ml] lemon juice, plus more as needed

1/2 cup [120 ml] organic extra-virgin olive oil or canola oil

Freshly ground black pepper

Place the garlic on a cutting board and smash with the flat side of a chef's knife. Sprinkle with 1/4 tsp salt. Use the knife to mince the garlic, then scrape it into a small pile and use the side of the knife to press the garlic and salt together. Repeat the process until the garlic and salt form a paste.

Place the garlic paste in a small bowl and add the mustard. Whisk in the lemon juice, then slowly whisk in the olive oil to combine. Add a few grindings of pepper. Taste (I like to dip a piece of lettuce into the vinaigrette to taste), adding more salt, lemon juice, or Dijon as desired.

Store in an airtight glass container in the refrigerator for up to 1 week. Whisk again just before serving to re-emulsify.

CHIPOTLE-LIME VINAIGRETTE

Chipotles in adobo are responsible for that deep, smoky chile flavor in marinades, vinaigrettes, and some of my favorite Mexican braises. In this vinaigrette (pictured on page 53, in the beaker), it gives depth of flavor and pairs well with the lime juice and honey. I use a chipotle paste from the online store Art of the Chipotle instead of canned chipotles in adobo, which often have hidden gluten. The paste comes pureed and seedless. Plus, there is a screw cap so it lasts forever in the refrigerator. If you have canned chipotles, start with 2 tsp and work your way up with heat. If you are sensitive to nightshades, the Curried Black Pepper Vinaigrette (page 51) is for you.

PREPARATION TIME
10 minutes

MAKES
1¼ cups / 300 ml

½ cup [120 ml] lime juice

2 tsp to 2 Tbsp chipotle paste

1 Tbsp honey

2 garlic cloves, smashed and peeled

Kosher salt

½ cup [120 ml] organic canola oil

Freshly ground black pepper (optional)

Place the lime juice, 2 tsp of the chipotle paste, and the honey, garlic, and ½ tsp salt in a blender. Blend until combined. On low speed, slowly pour in the canola oil, blending until combined. Taste (I like to dip a piece of lettuce into the vinaigrette to taste), adding pepper or more salt or chipotle paste if desired.

Store in an airtight glass container in the refrigerator for up to 1 week. Shake just before serving to re-emulsify.

CLASSIC BASIL AND PINE NUT PESTO

Pesto is perfect for topping grilled meats, chicken, fish, or veggies and is easily tossed with pasta or grains for salads. I make pesto or chimichurri (see page 56) at least once a week. I have tried other versions of pesto and always find my way back to this traditional one, as it's just so good. I like to toast the pine nuts to bring out their nuttiness, but some traditionalists leave them untoasted. The pungency of basil can vary, so taste this sauce as you go. Sometimes I find that my pesto needs a generous pinch of salt at the end simply to add flavor, whereas other times the basil is so fragrant that I don't want to add any salt at all. This recipe makes enough to coat 2 lb [910 g] cooked pasta.

PREPARATION TIME
12 minutes

MAKES
1¼ cups / 300 ml

⅓ cup [50 g] pine nuts

⅓ cup [30 g] grated Parmigiano-Reggiano (optional)

1 garlic clove, peeled

3 cups [100 g] firmly packed basil leaves

¾ cup [180 ml] extra-virgin olive oil, plus more as needed

½ tsp kosher salt

Freshly ground black pepper

Warm a skillet over medium heat. Add the pine nuts and stir constantly until they are lightly browned, about 2 minutes. Transfer to a plate to cool.

Place the cooled pine nuts, Parmigiano-Reggiano (if using), and garlic in a food processor. Pulse a few times to break up the garlic. Add the basil and pulse an additional ten times. With the motor running, slowly pour in the olive oil and puree until the pesto is the texture of a coarse paste. Taste, stirring in the salt and a fresh grinding of black pepper. (If you'd like thinner pesto, stir in more oil or 2 to 3 Tbsp water.)

Store in an airtight container, topped with a thin layer of olive oil, in the refrigerator for up to 1 week.

CHIMICHURRI
with mint and basil

Heavy cream-and-flour-based sauces can be delicious, but healthier ingredients like herbs, vinegar, oil, and aromatics take center stage in my favorite sauces. Chimichurri (pictured opposite, top) is one of my go-to's. Hailing from Argentina where it is paired with grilled skirt steak, this green sauce is a lively addition to practically everything. My family likes to spoon it over salmon and use it as a dip for roasted veggies. I love the herb combo in the recipe, but use whatever you have. Both cilantro and chives can be thrown in the mix.

PREPARATION TIME
10 minutes

MAKES
1¼ cups / 300 ml

3 Tbsp sherry vinegar

1 Tbsp Dijon mustard

3 garlic cloves, peeled

2 cups [40 g] loosely packed parsley leaves

1 cup [20 g] loosely packed basil leaves

1 cup [20 g] loosely packed mint leaves

¾ cup [180 ml] extra-virgin olive oil

Kosher salt (optional)

Place the vinegar, mustard, and garlic in the bowl of a food processor. Pulse a few times to break up the garlic. Add all the herbs and pulse until the herbs are evenly chopped. Use a spatula to scrape down the sides of the bowl, then add the olive oil. Pulse until the herbs are coarsely chopped and a thick sauce forms. (For a thinner sauce, stir in additional oil.) Taste, adding salt if desired.

Store in an airtight container in the refrigerator for up to 1 week.

no food processor or blender?

Make these green sauces directly on a cutting board. Roughly chop the garlic with the Dijon mustard, add the herbs, and chop to reach the desired consistency. Transfer to a small bowl and pour in the oil and vinegar, then stir with a spoon to incorporate. Season with salt and serve.

ROMESCO
with toasted almonds and mint

I can't remember the first time I had the Catalonian sauce romesco, but like its cousins, chimichurri from Argentina and pesto from Italy, it seems to have a permanent spot in my refrigerator. I've opted out of using bread in my version (pictured on page 57, bottom), leaving more room for the ingredients that make me feel great—almonds, mint, and olive oil. Serve romesco as a dip with roasted fingerling potatoes or grilled veggies, or let it shine on a grilled steak or piece of fish. (Or just eat it with a spoon.) Red bell peppers have twice as much vitamin C as green ones. If you're sensitive to nightshades, stick to pesto (see page 55) and chimichurri (see page 56).

PREPARATION TIME
25 minutes

COOKING TIME
30 minutes

MAKES
2 cups / 480 ml

---

4 red bell peppers

5 Tbsp [80 ml] extra-virgin olive oil

Kosher salt

¼ cup [30 g] slivered almonds

2 garlic cloves, peeled and coarsely chopped

1 shallot, sliced

¼ tsp crushed red pepper

1 Tbsp sherry vinegar

Freshly ground black pepper

2 Tbsp chopped mint

½ lemon

Place a rack in the top third of the oven and preheat the oven to 400°F [200°C]. Line a baking sheet with parchment paper.

Place the bell peppers in a medium bowl. Drizzle with 1 Tbsp of the olive oil, sprinkle with a generous pinch of salt, and toss until the peppers are well coated. Transfer to the prepared baking sheet. Roast for 15 minutes, turn the peppers, and continue roasting until the peppers are charred and soft, with their skins beginning to peel away, an additional 20 minutes. Transfer the peppers to a large bowl, cover tightly with plastic wrap, and let sit for 10 minutes. When the peppers are cool enough to handle, remove the stems, skin, and seeds. Cut the flesh into rough strips and set aside.

In a medium skillet over medium heat, cook the almonds, stirring constantly, until they begin to look and smell toasted, about 4 minutes. Place them on a plate to cool.

Add 2 Tbsp of the olive oil to the same pan, then add the garlic, shallot, and crushed red pepper. Cook, stirring constantly, until the garlic just begins to cook and the shallot softens, about 2 minutes.

Place the roasted peppers and sautéed garlic and shallot in the bowl of a food processor. Pulse a few times, then add the toasted almonds. Pulse a few more times, scraping down the sides of the bowl with a spatula if necessary, then add the remaining 2 Tbsp olive oil, the sherry vinegar, ¼ tsp salt, and a few grinds of pepper. Process until the romesco is uniformly pureed but retains some texture, similar to a pesto sauce.

Transfer to a small airtight container. Stir in the mint, a squeeze of lemon juice, and a few grinds of pepper. Taste and season with additional salt and pepper if desired.

Store in the refrigerator for up to 1 week.

why roast peppers whole?

Bell peppers retain more of their moisture when roasted whole. They may take a little longer but it's worth it.

PEPERONATA

My family has taken to eating this peperonata with a spoon while it's still in the pan. I've started doubling the recipe to be safe. It elevates any fish and is delicious with roasted chicken, too. If you're sensitive to nightshades, turn to caramelized onions (see page 62) instead.

PREPARATION TIME
15 minutes

COOKING TIME
50 minutes

MAKES
4 cups / 840 g

3 red bell peppers

2 yellow bell peppers

5 Tbsp [80 ml] extra-virgin olive oil, plus more for finishing (optional)

Kosher salt

1 yellow onion, thinly sliced

1 small fennel bulb, core and stems removed, thinly sliced

3 garlic cloves, peeled and minced

1/4 tsp crushed red pepper

2 Tbsp capers, rinsed and drained

2 Tbsp sherry vinegar

Freshly ground black pepper

Place a rack in the top third of the oven and preheat the oven to 400°F [200°C]. Line a baking sheet with parchment paper.

Place all the bell peppers in a medium bowl. Drizzle with 1 Tbsp of the olive oil, sprinkle with a generous pinch of salt, and toss until the peppers are well coated. Transfer to the prepared baking sheet. Roast for 15 minutes, turn the peppers, and continue roasting until the peppers are charred and soft, with their skins beginning to peel away, an additional 20 minutes. Return the peppers to a medium bowl, cover tightly with plastic wrap, and let sit for 10 minutes. When the peppers are cool enough to handle, remove the stems, skin, and seeds. Cut the flesh into rough strips and set aside.

In a large sauté pan over medium heat, warm the remaining 4 Tbsp [60 ml] olive oil. Add the onion and fennel and cook, stirring occasionally, until softened, 8 to 10 minutes. Add the garlic, crushed red pepper, and $1/2$ tsp salt and cook, stirring constantly, until fragrant, about 1 minute. Stir in the capers and vinegar and allow the vinegar to reduce for 1 minute. Remove from the heat. Stir in the roasted peppers.

Transfer to an airtight container. Taste and adjust the salt and pepper as desired. If using, finish with a generous drizzle of extra-virgin olive oil.

Store in the refrigerator for up to 1 week.

CARAMELIZED ONIONS

My favorite method for preparing onions is caramelizing them. Cooking them very slowly over low heat brings out all their sugars, leaving you with the perfect condiment to fold into scrambled eggs, toss in a pasta, whisk into a vinaigrette, or serve as a side with grilled chicken or fish. I always do a huge batch, as three onions cook down to about 2¼ cups [120 g]. You can easily prepare leeks or shallots following my method for onions, but they cook much faster, 8 to 10 minutes total.

PREPARATION TIME
10 minutes

COOKING TIME
55 minutes

MAKES
2¼ cups / 120 g

---

3 Tbsp olive oil

---

3 large yellow onions, thinly sliced

---

1 tsp kosher salt

In a large sauté pan over medium-low heat, warm the olive oil. Add the onions and salt and cook, stirring often, until the onions start to wilt, about 10 minutes. When the onions begin to caramelize, stir frequently, scraping the browned bits from the bottom on the pan so the natural sugars do not burn. Continue to cook, stirring frequently, until the onions are a deep brown, about 45 minutes.

Store in an airtight container in the refrigerator for up to 3 days.

time saver

You can shave 15 to 20 minutes off the cooking time if you are willing to turn up the heat and stir the onions constantly. Just do not walk away. A minute without attention means burned onions.

PICKLED ONIONS

I'll eat anything that's pickled, but these onions take the cake. Making a batch on the weekends creates endless opportunities for topping fish tacos, scrambled eggs, or black beans, or even mixing them into salads. If you are sensitive to nightshades, omit the jalapeño.

PREPARATION TIME
10 minutes

COOKING TIME
2 hours of "pickling"

MAKES
2 cups / 300 g

½ cup [120 ml] lime juice

¼ cup [60 ml] warm water

1 tsp raw cane sugar

½ tsp kosher salt

1 red onion, halved and thinly sliced

1 jalapeño, sliced (optional if nightshade-sensitive)

Place the lime juice, water, sugar, and salt in a medium bowl and whisk to dissolve the salt. Submerge the onion and jalapeño (if using) in the liquid. Allow them to sit for 2 hours until slightly pickled.

Store in an airtight container in the refrigerator for up to 1 week.

CANNELLINI BEANS
with garlic and herbs

The secret to these beans is to cook them low and slow. Enjoy on their own as an entrée, alongside steak or roasted vegetables, or spread on toast.

PREPARATION TIME
10 minutes
(plus 1 hour for quick soaking or up to overnight soaking)

COOKING TIME
about 2 hours

SERVES
8

---

2 cups [330 g] cannellini or white navy beans

½ cup [120 ml] extra-virgin olive oil

2 garlic cloves, peeled and chopped

1 rosemary sprig

2 thyme sprigs

Kosher salt

Spread the beans on a baking sheet and discard any small stones or broken beans. Place the beans in a large Dutch oven or heavy stockpot and cover with water by 2 in [5 cm]. Allow to soak overnight, then drain the beans and refill the pot to cover the beans with water by 2 in [5 cm]. Alternatively, to quick soak the beans, cover with water by 2 in [5 cm]. Bring to a boil over high heat, then immediately turn off the heat and put the lid on the pot. Allow to sit for 1 hour, then drain the beans and refill the pot to cover the beans with water by 2 in [5 cm].

Bring the beans to a boil, then lower the heat and simmer partially covered until the beans are just tender to the bite, 1½ to 2 hours. If the beans are older, you may need to add more boiling water to keep them covered and cook a bit longer.

When the beans are done, reserve 1½ cups [360 ml] of the cooking liquid, then drain the beans. Rinse out the pot and place over low heat. Add the olive oil, garlic, and herbs and cook, stirring occasionally, until the garlic begins to cook through but is not crispy, 2 to 3 minutes. Stir in the beans, half of the reserved cooking liquid, and ½ tsp salt. Simmer for 15 minutes. Taste, adding more salt if desired, and the rest of the cooking liquid if you'd like a more spreadable, creamy texture.

Store in an airtight container in the refrigerator for up to 1 week.

CHIPOTLE BLACK BEANS

As food prices soar, I have begun to appreciate beans as a staple. Use these as the base for breakfast bowls (see page 84) or in your favorite tacos, or garnish them with freshly shaved radish, cabbage, and Cotija cheese as an entrée.

PREPARATION TIME
15 minutes
(plus 4–12 hours for soaking)

COOKING TIME
1¼ – 2 hours

SERVES
10

2 cups [370 g] dried black beans

3 Tbsp extra-virgin olive oil

1 red onion, diced

1 jalapeño, diced (optional if nightshade-sensitive)

2 garlic cloves, peeled and minced

1 Tbsp chili powder

1 tsp ground cumin

½ tsp dried oregano

2 Tbsp chipotles in adobo (optional if nightshade-sensitive)

¼ cup [60 ml] lime juice

Kosher salt

Spread the beans on a baking sheet and discard any small stones or broken beans. Place the beans in a Dutch oven or heavy stockpot and cover with water by 2 in [5 cm]. Allow to sit for at least 4 hours, or up to overnight. Drain the beans and set aside.

Place the same pot over medium heat. When it is hot, add the olive oil, onion, and jalapeño (if using). Cook, stirring occasionally, until the onion is soft, 5 to 7 minutes. Add the garlic and cook for 1 minute until fragrant. Add the chili powder, cumin, and oregano and stir until fragrant, about 1 minute. Stir in the beans, chipotles, and 6 cups [1.4 L] water. Bring to a simmer, cover partially, and cook until the beans are tender, 1 to 1½ hours depending on the age of the beans. Stir in the lime juice and 1 tsp salt, then taste and add more salt if desired.

Store in an airtight container in the refrigerator for up to 1 week.

BASIC QUINOA

After a lot of practice, I have learned to love quinoa. It now takes center stage as a salad (see page 124), shaped into a cake and fried in olive oil for a crispy little base for eggs (see page 89), and even as a starter for a breakfast stir-fry. Remember, you must always rinse quinoa before cooking it to wash away the coating of saponins, a naturally occurring pesticide that many people identify as having a bitter taste. Rinsing makes all the difference in the final flavor. For a fancier version, sauté a minced shallot in olive oil until soft, about 2 minutes, before adding the quinoa.

PREPARATION TIME
5 minutes

COOKING TIME
20 minutes

SERVES
8–10

2 cups [340 g] organic white or red quinoa

4 cups [960 ml] chicken broth, vegetable broth, or water

Pinch of kosher salt

In a fine-mesh strainer, rinse the quinoa well under cold running water and drain. In a medium saucepan over high heat, bring the chicken broth and salt to a boil. Stir in the quinoa, cover, and turn the heat to medium-low. Simmer until the quinoa is tender and white quinoa tails are visible, about 18 minutes. Transfer to a shallow bowl or baking sheet and set aside to cool to room temperature. Fluff with a fork, and then serve.

how to cool quinoa

Cool quinoa completely before refrigerating. To cool quinoa quickly, spread it out onto a baking sheet. Store in an airtight container in the refrigerator for up to 1 week.

ALMOND MILK

I love dairy. But when I discovered I was gluten intolerant, I learned that many people who are gluten sensitive are also sensitive to lactose. So I eliminated dairy from my diet to see what would happen. Immediately my eczema—something I've had all my life—went away. I try to use healthful alternatives, such as nut milks, as much as possible. Nut milks are now the base of my smoothies and the addition to my coffee or tea.

I'd been buying almond milk for years before I discovered how much better it tasted when I made it myself. With almonds, it's important to soak them overnight. Soaking them in purified water releases the phytic acid, tannins, and enzyme inhibitors, allowing your body to access more of the nuts' amazing nutrients. It helps to change the water every 3 or 4 hours, too.

PREPARATION TIME
15 minutes
(plus 12 hours soaking time)

MAKES
4 cups / 960 ml

2 cups [270 g] organic raw almonds, skin on

Purified water to cover, plus 4½ cups [1 L]

1 to 2 tsp vanilla extract (optional)

1 tsp maple syrup (optional)

½ tsp sea salt (optional)

Place the almonds in a medium bowl and cover with purified water by 2 in [5 cm]. Cover and let sit at room temperature for 12 hours. Drain the almonds, then place them in a blender along with the 4½ cups [1 L] purified water. Blend on high speed until very smooth, about 2 minutes. There will still be some pulp left.

Working in two batches, pour the liquid through a fine-mesh strainer set over a small bowl. Using the back of a wooden spoon or ladle, press down on the almond pulp to extract as much of the milk as possible. Discard the pulp, and then repeat with the rest of the liquid. Repeat the straining process as necessary to reach the desired texture. Taste and stir in the vanilla, maple syrup, or salt, if desired.

Store in an airtight container in the refrigerator for up to 1 week. Stir before each use.

CINNAMON CASHEW MILK

Unlike almonds, cashews do not need to be soaked, making them a practical choice when you are in a hurry.

PREPARATION TIME
10 minutes

MAKES
5¼ cups / 1.3 L

1½ cups [200 g] organic raw cashew pieces

4½ cups [1 L] purified water

1 tsp maple syrup, plus more as needed

½ tsp ground cinnamon

Kosher salt

Place the cashews, purified water, maple syrup, and cinnamon in a blender. Blend on high speed until the nuts are thoroughly pureed and look like milk, about 1 minute. Pour the liquid through a fine-mesh strainer set over a small bowl to remove any pieces of cashew. Stir in a pinch of salt. Taste, adding more maple syrup or salt if desired.

Store in an airtight container in the refrigerator for up to 1 week. Stir before each use.

how to store nuts

Store all whole nuts in airtight containers in the freezer indefinitely to protect them from turning rancid.

THE PERFECT POACHED EGG

I eat poached eggs at least three days a week. I eat them on their own, or over a bowl of stir-fried quinoa and vegetables. We all have methods for poaching eggs, but I much prefer this one. The tools are important. A slotted spoon, a shallow sauté pan, ramekins, and a paper towel–lined plate are the keys to success.

PREPARATION TIME
10 minutes

COOKING TIME
3 minutes

SERVES
1

1 Tbsp white vinegar

1 tsp kosher salt

1 fresh egg

Fill a small, shallow sauté pan with 1½ in [4 cm] water. Bring to a simmer, then add the vinegar and salt. Lower the temperature so the water is barely bubbling. You should see small bubbles rising to the surface rather than large bubbles popping on top. A rolling boil will cook the eggs too quickly.

Crack the egg into a small bowl or ramekin. (If the yolk breaks, cover the egg with plastic wrap and refrigerate to save for another use.) Gently tip the egg into the water. Cook until the white is barely opaque and the yolk is still runny inside, about 3 minutes.

Using a slotted spoon, gently lift the egg out of the water and place on a paper towel–lined plate. Use the towel to pat off any extra water, then transfer the egg to a dry dish. Serve immediately.

how to shock poached eggs

If making poached eggs ahead and not serving them immediately, shock the cooked eggs in a bowl of ice water to stop the cooking. Transfer the ice-water bath and eggs to the refrigerator, and refrigerate for up to 8 hours. To rewarm the eggs, slip them into simmering water and heat for 15 to 30 seconds. Lift them into a strainer to drain, then slide onto a serving plate.

chapter

2

JUICES, SMOOTHIES, AND BREAKFASTS

When I discovered I was gluten intolerant, I realized breakfast was my biggest opportunity for improvement. For the most important meal of the day, I was filling my tank with the wrong kind of fuel. Whether or not you have a sensitivity to gluten, walking out the door on a stomach of refined flour, which causes blood sugar spikes and crashes before lunch, is not an optimal choice. Here are recipes chock-full of ingredients that will sustain you throughout the day while filling you with key anti-inflammatory ingredients like fruit, nuts, a few greens, and a few superfoods. They're also free of trans fats, low in saturated fats, and naturally gluten-free. With these recipes in my stomach, I have better concentration and energy throughout the morning.

A note about "drinking your vitamins": Juice cleansing, fasting, and meal replacement diets are commonplace today. For me, drinking fresh juices and smoothies is not a meal replacement strategy. Instead, I use juices and whole-food smoothies as an effective way to pack additional nutrients into my diet. In order to make fruit and vegetable drinks a real part of my breakfasts, I've learned to prep everything the night before so it's ready to go in the morning. I also invested in two pieces of equipment that haven't failed me yet: a high-powered juicer and a high-powered blender. Their consistent results make my fruits and vegetables taste amazing every time.

BEGINNER GREEN JUICE

This juice (pictured opposite, top) is for those of you just starting out. It's sweeter than other versions but is still loaded with powerful greens.

PREPARATION TIME
15 minutes

MAKES
4¼ cups / 1 L

2 celery stalks

2 Granny Smith apples

2 cucumbers

2 hearts of romaine lettuce

1 bunch lacinato kale, stems removed

½ bunch parsley

One 1-in [2.5-cm] piece of fresh ginger

1 lemon or lime

Wash all the fruits and vegetables and pat dry. Juice the celery, apples, cucumbers, lettuce, kale, parsley, and ginger according to your juicer's instructions. Squeeze in the lemon juice and stir. Serve immediately.

quick kale prep

There is no need to use a knife when removing kale leaves from the stems. Hold the leaf of kale at the stem with one hand and use your other to pull the leaf from the bottom of the stem upward. You'll wind up with the stem in one hand and leaves in the other. If you're like me, you can't help but think about the waste inherent in juicing (all that left-behind fiber!). I get more yield out of my kale by rolling the leaves around quartered apples and then putting them through the juicer.

ADVANCED GREEN JUICE

A friend of mine who juices daily told me to focus on the 80/20 rule: 80 percent greens and 20 percent fruit. I've made this juice (pictured on page 75, bottom) even better by adding turmeric. Combining spinach, cucumber, and fennel in one drink is an ideal way to get a variety of green vegetables into your diet.

PREPARATION TIME
15 minutes

MAKES
1½ cups / 360 ml

3 cups [120 g] spinach

1 Granny Smith apple

1 cucumber

1 fennel bulb

One 1-in [2.5-cm] piece of fresh ginger

One 1-in [2.5-cm] piece of fresh turmeric

Freshly ground black pepper

1 lemon

Wash all the fruits and vegetables and pat dry. Juice the spinach, apple, cucumber, fennel, ginger, turmeric, and a pinch of pepper according to your juicer's instructions. Squeeze in the lemon juice and stir. Serve immediately, garnished with another pinch of pepper.

PINEAPPLE, MINT, AND CUCUMBER JUICE

When I drink this juice, I feel like I'm doing something great for my body. Must be all of the manganese, vitamin C, and B vitamins in the pineapple! The cucumber adds clean flavor to the sweet fruit, and the mint adds balance.

PREPARATION TIME
10 minutes

MAKES
3½ cups / 840 ml

1 large, ripe pineapple, skin removed and core intact

¼ cup [7 g] mint leaves

1 cucumber

Cut the pineapple in long strips that will fit through the juicer feed tube. Process the pineapple, adding the mint leaves in between pieces, on the proper setting of the juicer. Juice the cucumber, then stir. Serve immediately.

how to cut pineapple

To peel a pineapple, cut off both ends and place the pineapple on end on a cutting board. With a serrated knife, cut lengthwise down the pineapple, removing just enough skin to take away the eyes. Turning the pineapple, continue cutting off the skin.

ACAI AND MIXED BERRY SMOOTHIE

Smoothies are often loaded with refined sugar, which eliminates the health benefits associated with them. By using frozen fruit instead of juice or sorbet, you get just enough sweetness without the added sugar. In my favorite purple smoothie, frozen fruit fills in for ice, lending a creamy texture while preventing the drink from getting diluted. Luckily, acai berry puree is sold in convenient little packs in the freezer section. Because the berries have soft skins that easily absorb pesticides, purchasing organic is a must. Frozen organic fruit like mango is readily available and is fairly close in price to the nonorganic equivalent.

PREPARATION TIME
10 minutes

MAKES
3½ cups / 840 ml

One 3.5-oz [100-g] pack frozen acai puree

1 cup [120 g] frozen mango chunks

1 cup [120 g] frozen berries, such as blueberries and/or raspberries

2 cups [480 ml] Cinnamon Cashew Milk (page 70) or Almond Milk (page 68)

1 to 2 tsp maple syrup or honey (optional)

Under hot water, defrost the acai pack to soften. Place the acai, mango, and berries in a blender, along with the nut milk. Starting on a low setting, puree the mixture until it begins to break up, stopping and scraping down the sides if necessary. Slowly turn the blender speed to high and puree until there are no lumps, 1 to 2 minutes. Taste and blend in the maple syrup, if desired. Serve immediately.

save the leftovers!

Freeze leftover smoothie in ice-cube trays. When you're ready to make another smoothie, simply pop a few cubes into your blender.

CRANBERRY-ORANGE GRANOLA
with toasted pecans

Homemade granola allows me to control the sweetness while pumping up the mixture with anti-inflammatory ingredients such as flaxseed meal, nuts, and dried cranberries. Coconut oil, maple syrup, and dried fruit are laden with calories, so keep this granola as a topping for yogurt or have an actual portion size ($\frac{1}{3}$ cup [50 g]) instead of a bowlful.

PREPARATION TIME
10 minutes

COOKING TIME
30–40 minutes

MAKES
4 $\frac{2}{3}$ cups / 600 g

---

3 cups [300 g] gluten-free rolled oats, such as Bob's Red Mill

---

2 Tbsp flaxseed meal

$\frac{1}{3}$ cup [80 ml] maple syrup

$\frac{1}{4}$ cup [40 g] fresh-pressed coconut oil

---

1 orange, washed

$\frac{3}{4}$ cup [80 g] chopped pecans, toasted (see below)

$\frac{1}{2}$ cup [60 g] juice-sweetened dried cranberries

Preheat the oven to 300°F [150°C].

Place the oats and flaxseed meal in a large bowl.

In a small saucepan over low heat, combine the maple syrup and coconut oil. Zest the orange peel directly into the syrup, then cut the orange in half and squeeze 2 Tbsp juice into the pan. Stir just until the coconut oil has melted, about 3 minutes, then remove from the heat. Pour the maple syrup over the oats and stir to coat.

Spread the oats evenly onto a baking sheet. Bake for 15 minutes, then stir. Bake for another 10 minutes, then stir in the pecans and cranberries. Bake until the oats are golden and the berries are plumped, another 5 to 10 minutes. Set aside to cool completely.

Store in an airtight container at room temperature for up to 5 days.

how to toast nuts and seeds

To toast any type of nut or seed quickly, warm a skillet over medium heat. Once the skillet is hot, add the nuts and stir constantly until they're browned and fragrant, 4 to 5 minutes.

GARLICKY TOFU SCRAMBLE
with green onions and herb salad

My son Charlie recently asked to mess around in the kitchen while I was working on this book. I reluctantly agreed, knowing that he'd be in my way making a mess. But he ended up combining a few things I never would have, and I found myself eating this recipe directly out of the pan. His biggest tip? The tofu needs to be really dry. Drain it, cut it in half cross-wise, and place paper towels over and under it. Then press down on the tofu with the paper towels to extract and absorb the water. You might need to do this a few times before dicing the tofu.

Charlie, thank you for reminding me that sometimes creativity just has to happen!

PREPARATION TIME	COOKING TIME	SERVES
10 minutes	8 minutes	4

3 Tbsp fresh-pressed coconut oil or extra-virgin olive oil

3 green onions, white and green parts, thinly sliced on the bias

3 garlic cloves, peeled and thinly sliced

One 15-oz [430-g] package firm tofu, thoroughly drained and diced into ½-in [12-mm] pieces

Kosher salt

1 cup [90 g] mung bean sprouts

2 Tbsp chopped mint

2 Tbsp chopped parsley

1 Tbsp lime juice, plus more as needed

Fish sauce for serving (optional)

Cooked brown rice for serving (optional)

Poached eggs (see page 71) for serving (optional)

Place the coconut oil, white parts of the green onions, and garlic in a cold sauté pan. Turn the heat to low. As the aromatics warm, stir occasionally until they are lightly browned and softened, about 4 minutes.

Add the tofu and a pinch of salt and turn the heat to medium. Cook, stirring occasionally, until the tofu is well coated with the oil and warmed, about 3 minutes. Stir in the mung bean sprouts and warm for 1 minute. Add the green parts of the green onions and the mint, parsley, and lime juice. Stir to combine. Taste, adding fish sauce or additional lime juice, if desired.

Serve the scramble on its own, or over brown rice with poached eggs on top.

BLACK BEAN BOWLS
with Avocado Mash and Pico de Gallo

Starting my day out with a sweet pastry and a cup of coffee is a recipe for a blood sugar crash by 10 A.M. I haven't let go of the coffee, but cooking a quick breakfast that has fiber, protein, and some greens is the way I get through the morning. If you've made a pot of black beans (see page 66) for the week, they're delicious here. Otherwise canned black beans that have been rinsed work well, too. If you're sensitive to nightshades, substitute mango for the cherry tomatoes.

PREPARATION TIME
35 minutes

COOKING TIME
5–10 minutes

SERVES
4

PICO DE GALLO

2 cups [330 g] cherry tomatoes, halved (optional if nightshade-sensitive), or diced mango

1 jalapeño, minced (optional if nightshade-sensitive)

2 Tbsp chopped cilantro

2 Tbsp finely diced white onion

1 Tbsp lime juice

Kosher salt (optional)

AVOCADO MASH

2 avocados

Kosher salt

1 Tbsp finely diced white onion

1 Tbsp lime juice

1 to 2 dashes of hot sauce

One 15-oz [425-g] can black beans, rinsed and drained

1 Tbsp lime juice

Kosher salt

4 eggs, poached (see page 71) or scrambled

Hot sauce for serving

To make the pico de gallo: Combine the tomatoes (if using), jalapeño (if using), cilantro, onion, and lime juice in a small bowl. Taste, adding salt if desired, and stir to mix.

To make the avocado mash: Place the avocados in a small bowl or molcajete with a generous sprinkling of salt. Using a fork or pastry blender, mash until the avacados are a bit chunky or completely smooth, depending on your preference. Stir in the onion, lime juice, and hot sauce. Taste, adding more salt or more hot sauce if needed.

In a small saucepan, warm the black beans and lime juice, mash gently with a fork, and season with salt.

Place one-fourth of the black beans in each bowl, then one-fourth of the avocado mash. Top with an egg, then the pico de gallo and a dash of hot sauce. Serve immediately.

BREAKFAST BIBIMBAP
with poached eggs

Most mornings at work, you'll find me up in our test kitchen making breakfast before anyone else arrives. While I unload the dishwasher, I bring a pan of water to a boil for poaching my eggs, then rummage through the refrigerator for something green to throw in another pan, along with leftover quinoa or brown rice. After just a few minutes of sizzle, the perfect breakfast is ready! I realized that I've been riffing on bibimbap, the classic Korean dish that means "mixed rice." You can use whatever veggies you have on hand to make this breakfast: spinach, kale, mung bean sprouts, mushrooms . . . the combinations are endless.

PREPARATION TIME
30 minutes

COOKING TIME
15 minutes

SERVES
4

4 tsp toasted sesame oil

1 carrot, peeled and cut into ¼-in [6-mm] matchsticks

1 zucchini, cut into ¼-in [6-mm] matchsticks

3 green onions, white and light green parts only, thinly sliced

Kosher salt

2 cups [180 g] sliced mushrooms, such as shiitake and cremini

1 garlic clove, peeled and minced

2 cups [300 g] cooked brown rice or quinoa (see page 67)

1 Tbsp chopped basil

1 Tbsp chopped mint

1 tsp toasted sesame seeds

4 poached eggs (see page 71)

Hot sauce, such as Sriracha, for serving (optional)

CONTINUED

In a large nonstick skillet over medium-high heat, warm 1 tsp of the sesame oil. Add the carrot, zucchini, and green onions, along with a pinch of salt. Cook, stirring frequently, until the vegetables have just browned and are crisp-tender, about 3 minutes. Remove the vegetables from the pan.

Place the pan back over medium-high heat, add another 1 tsp sesame oil and allow the pan to get very hot. Add the mushrooms in one layer. Allow them to sit and get a nice crust before stirring, about 3 minutes, then add the garlic. Cook, stirring frequently, until the mushrooms have released their liquid and are well browned, about 2 minutes more. Remove the mushrooms from the pan.

Place the pan back over medium-high heat and add the remaining 2 tsp sesame oil. Allow the pan to get very hot, then add the brown rice and spread it over the bottom of the pan. Let it crisp before breaking it up and stirring, about 2 minutes. Stir, then spread the rice over the bottom of the pan again and allow to crisp for 2 minutes more.

Divide the rice between four bowls and top each serving with vegetables, fresh herbs, sesame seeds, and a poached egg. Add as much hot sauce as desired. Serve immediately!

BREAKFAST QUINOA CAKES

This idea came to my talented test-kitchen cook Melissa Stewart when she was thinking about a gluten-free alternative to the English muffin. The finished texture is total nostalgia. It reminds us of fried hash brown patties but is certainly a more healthful option. You can use the quinoa cakes for a breakfast stack—topped with sautéed greens and a poached egg. They would also make a delicious substitution for the traditional starch or grain side dish.

PREPARATION TIME
20 minutes

COOKING TIME
30 minutes

SERVES
4

1 cup [85 g] organic tri-color quinoa

2 tsp extra-virgin olive oil, plus 4 Tbsp [60 ml]

1 tsp minced garlic or ½ tsp roasted garlic powder

3 Tbsp finely diced shallot or 1 tsp dried minced onion

2 eggs

½ cup [60 g] chickpea flour

½ tsp ground dry mustard

1 tsp kosher salt

⅛ tsp freshly ground black pepper

⅛ tsp cayenne pepper

2 Tbsp chopped fresh parsley or 1 tsp dried parsley

1 Tbsp chopped fresh chives or 1 tsp dried chives

CONTINUED

In a fine-mesh strainer, rinse the quinoa well under cold running water and drain. In a small saucepan over high heat, bring 1³/₄ cups [420 ml] water to a boil. Stir in the quinoa, cover, and turn the heat to medium-low. Simmer until the quinoa is tender and white quinoa tails are visible, about 18 minutes. Transfer to a shallow bowl or baking sheet and set aside to cool to room temperature.

In a small sauté pan over medium heat, warm the 2 tsp olive oil. Add the minced garlic and diced shallot (if using dried, whisk into the egg mixture with the other seasonings) and cook, stirring frequently, until fragrant and softened, 2 to 3 minutes.

In a large bowl, whisk together the eggs, chickpea flour, dry mustard, salt, black pepper, cayenne, parsley, chives, and softened garlic and shallot. Fold in cooled quinoa and mix until thoroughly incorporated.

Divide the mixture into eight portions. Using your hands, form the portions into patties, place on a parchment paper–lined baking sheet, and pat to ¹/₂ in [12 mm] thick.

In a large nonstick sauté pan over medium heat, warm 2 Tbsp of the olive oil. Cook half of the patties until golden brown and crispy, 3 to 4 minutes per side. Add the remaining 2 Tbsp oil and cook the rest of the patties. Serve immediately.

make the quinoa ahead

The quinoa mixture can be made up to 2 days ahead. Transfer to a covered container and refrigerate until ready to use.

TURKEY-CRANBERRY SAUSAGE
with sage

I love starting my day with a lot of protein, and in an effort to stop eating bacon, I've looked to other sources. These turkey sausages are a total treat. There is no need to add bread to bind the ingredients, and the clean flavors of lemon zest and sage are delicious together. You can freeze some of the patties and cook them later if you like. Don't second-guess my instruction to cook them over medium-low heat. I've learned my lesson from cranking up the heat and scorching them. Patience . . .

PREPARATION TIME
20 minutes
(plus 1 hour or up to overnight resting time)

COOKING TIME
15–20 minutes

SERVES
6

2 tsp organic canola oil, plus 2 Tbsp

½ cup [70 g] finely chopped yellow onion

1½ lb [680 g] ground turkey

¾ cup [100 g] dried berries, such as cranberries, blueberries, or cherries

¼ cup [10 g] flat-leaf parsley leaves, chopped

1 egg, lightly beaten

1 Tbsp minced fresh sage

1 Tbsp thyme leaves

1 tsp grated lemon zest

1 tsp kosher salt

½ tsp ground black pepper

½ tsp ground allspice

In a small skillet over medium heat, warm the 2 tsp canola oil. Add the onion and cook, stirring frequently, until soft, 6 to 8 minutes. Let cool.

In a large bowl, combine cooked onion, ground turkey, dried berries, parsley, egg, sage, thyme, lemon zest, salt, pepper, and allspice. Stir gently to combine, being careful not to overmix. Cover and refrigerate the mixture for at least 1 hour, or up to overnight.

Shape the mixture into 12 patties, each about 2½ in [6 cm] wide and ½ in [12 mm] thick.

In a large nonstick skillet over medium-low heat, warm the 2 Tbsp canola oil. Arrange the patties in the pan so they are not touching (you will probably have to do two batches) and cook until they are browned and no longer pink in the center, 3 to 4 minutes per side. Serve immediately, or keep warm in a 200°F [95°C] oven for up to 30 minutes.

quick thyme prep

To strip thyme leaves off their woody stems, simply hold the top of a thyme sprig with one hand. Use the index finger and thumb on the other hand to pinch the sprig and pull straight down. You'll be left with the stem in one hand and the leaves on the cutting board.

chapter

3

SNACKS AND APPETIZERS

Snacks account for 25 percent of our daily caloric intake, yet they tend to be full of the refined ingredients that cause inflammation. Just go to the grocery store and read the list of ingredients on a box of crackers, a cereal bar, or even a so-called health bar. It is impossible to find a snack that doesn't contribute to inflammation let alone one that actually helps fight inflammation. I decided to take snacks seriously and make them count. I want snacks that taste great but fill me and my family enough to get us through the day's last push for work, sports, and homework. I also need recipes for those nights when the kids are milling around while I'm cooking, telling me they're so hungry and they can't wait for dinner to be ready. This is my favorite assortment of snacks and appetizers. Half snacks on the run, half easy appetizer ideas, these recipes are bound to get you through to dinner.

When I share this strategy with others, I'm often asked if we load up on snacks and spoil our appetite for dinner. My answer is simple: If we're all filling up on these superhealthful small bites, who cares? Just eat less for dinner and have left-overs for the next day.

CINNAMON-SPICED APPLE CHIPS

I'm obsessed with this crispy snack. They're so easy to make when you're doing other things around the house. After you take them out of the oven, give them a few minutes to crisp up as they cool down. You may omit the sugar entirely; if you do so, triple the cinnamon and lightly dust the apple slices with it. Pears work, too. They wind up with a texture a bit more like fruit leather—chewy and satisfying.

PREPARATION TIME
15 minutes

COOKING TIME
1 hour

MAKES
2 cups / 40 g

2 Tbsp raw cane sugar

1 tsp ground cinnamon

2 Granny Smith apples, cored and thinly sliced

Preheat the oven to 275°F [135°C]. Line two baking sheets with parchment paper.

Combine the sugar and cinnamon in a small bowl. Place the apple slices on the prepared baking sheet and sprinkle with the cinnamon-sugar mixture.

Bake until dehydrated and lightly browned, about 1 hour. Remove from the baking sheet and allow to cool until crispy, about 15 minutes.

Store in an airtight container at room temperature for up to 1 week.

KALE CHIPS

Kale chips are all the rage, but the prepared ones are outrageously expensive. Add a splash of olive oil and a little salt to kale leaves, and—voilà!—you've made an expensive snack affordable. I like mine plain, but you can add a few different things before baking: a pinch of red pepper flakes, chili powder and lime juice, or grated Parmesan cheese.

PREPARATION TIME
15 minutes

COOKING TIME
14–16 minutes

MAKES
4 cups / 80 g

1 bunch lacinato kale, rinsed, thoroughly dried, and stems removed

1 to 2 Tbsp olive oil

¼ tsp sea salt

Preheat the oven to 350°F [180°C].

Cut or tear the kale leaves into 2-in [5-cm] pieces and then place them in a large bowl. Add 1 Tbsp of the olive oil and the salt. Rub the leaves with your fingers, making sure they are well coated with the oil, adding up to another 1 Tbsp if necessary. Place the kale on two baking sheets, ensuring there is about 1 in [2.5 cm] between the leaves. If they're too close together, the leaves will steam instead of crisping.

Bake for 8 minutes. Remove from the oven and toss the leaves, then bake another 6 to 8 minutes until the leaves are crisp. Let cool.

Store in an airtight container at room temperature for up to 1 week.

PLANTAIN CHIPS

Although quite starchy, plantains are an excellent source of vitamins A, B$_6$, and C, and also rich in potassium—all important for keeping inflammation at bay. When baked instead of fried, they become a delicious, better-for-you option over corn or potato chips.

PREPARATION TIME
10 minutes

COOKING TIME
18–20 minutes

MAKES
2 cups / 400 g

2 lb [910 g] plantains, peeled and sliced thinly on the diagonal

¼ cup [60 ml] olive oil

½ tsp smoked paprika

½ tsp kosher salt

Preheat the oven to 375°F [190°C]. Line two baking sheets with parchment paper.

Lay the plantain slices in a single layer on the prepared baking sheets. Brush the tops of the slices with half of the olive oil, then turn them over and brush the other side with oil. Sprinkle with the paprika and salt.

Roast for 18 to 20 minutes, turning halfway through, until the plantains are golden and crunchy. Let cool completely.

Store in an airtight container at room temperature for up to 3 days.

SWEET AND SPICY PEPITAS

I get many of my ideas from the test-kitchen team at Williams-Sonoma. One of our cooks, Melissa Stewart, did a version of these to put in a spicy salad. I ate half of them before they ever left the baking sheet. In my version, I dial back the sugar and amp up the spice in order to add an extra boost of anti-inflammatory chiles.

PREPARATION TIME
10 minutes

COOKING TIME
25–30 minutes

MAKES
2 cups / 330 g

---

1 Tbsp chili powder

1 tsp ground cumin

Pinch of cayenne pepper

½ tsp kosher salt

¼ tsp freshly ground black pepper

1 Tbsp organic canola oil or grapeseed oil

3 Tbsp maple syrup

1 egg white

2 cups [330 g] raw pumpkin seeds

Preheat the oven to 300°F [150°C]. Line a baking sheet with parchment paper.

Combine the chili powder, cumin, cayenne, salt, and black pepper in a small bowl.

Whisk the canola oil, maple syrup, and egg white in a large bowl. Add the spices and stir to combine. Add the pumpkin seeds and toss to coat. Spread the mixture on the prepared baking sheet.

Bake, stirring once, for 25 to 30 minutes. Let cool on the baking sheet.

Store in an airtight container at room temperature for up to 3 days.

CURRY-SPICED NUT MIX
with maple and black pepper

I am always looking for new ways to incorporate anti-inflammatory ingredients into my snacks. With nuts, seeds, coconut oil, turmeric (in the curry powder), and black pepper, this spicy and slightly sweet mix is the perfect solution. I keep it at my desk and watch people sneak in to eat it.

PREPARATION TIME
10 minutes

COOKING TIME
30–35 minutes

MAKES
2 cups / 270 g

1 cup [130 g] raw cashew pieces

½ cup [70 g] raw macadamia nuts, roughly chopped

½ cup [70 g] raw pumpkin seeds

1 Tbsp fresh-pressed coconut oil

2 tsp maple syrup

2 tsp curry powder

½ tsp kosher salt

¼ tsp freshly ground black pepper

Pinch of cayenne pepper

Preheat the oven to 300°F [150°C]. Line a baking sheet with parchment paper.

Combine the cashews, macadamias, and pumpkin seeds in a large bowl.

In a medium saucepan over low heat, melt the coconut oil with the maple syrup, about 1 minute. Remove from the heat and pour over the nut mixture. Add the curry powder, salt, black pepper, and cayenne pepper and stir well to coat. Spread the mixture on the prepared baking sheet.

Bake, stirring once, until the nuts are light brown, 30 to 35 minutes. Let cool on the baking sheet.

Store in an airtight container at room temperature for up to 3 days.

DARK CHOCOLATE–CHERRY TRAIL MIX

Every time I send my kids to a sports practice with this trail mix, a parent says something like, "There she goes again, acting all Berkeley on us." We live over the hill from Berkeley, California, where the community focuses on the healthiest, organic food. With the proven benefits of almonds, pumpkin seeds, cherries, and dark chocolate all in one recipe, this mix provides an irresistible dose of inflammatory-fighting ingredients. Pack a few containers and hit the trail—any trail.

PREPARATION TIME
5 minutes

COOKING TIME
10 minutes

MAKES
4 cups / 560 g

1 cup [170 g] raw almonds

1 cup [170 g] raw pumpkin seeds, toasted (see page 81) or spiced

½ cup [70 g] raw pistachios

½ cup [100 g] dried cherries or cranberries

½ cup [90 g] dark chocolate chips

Preheat the oven to 350°F [180°C].

Place the almonds in a single layer on a baking sheet. Bake, stirring once, until the almonds are fragrant and beginning to brown, about 10 minutes. Let cool, then coarsely chop.

Place the chopped almonds, pumpkin seeds, pistachios, cherries, and chocolate chips in a large bowl and stir to combine.

Store in an airtight container at room temperature for up to 5 days.

HUMMUS
with pine nuts and parsley

Confession—I used to eat organic, store-bought hummus almost every day. I always feel good about myself when I eat it. It's hard to go wrong with chickpeas, olive oil, and garlic. I decided to make my own to see if it was that much better. The truth? You tell me! Serve with sliced cucumbers, if desired.

PREPARATION TIME
20 minutes

MAKES
2 cups / 480 g

Two 15-oz [425-g] cans chickpeas, drained and rinsed

3 Tbsp lemon juice, plus more as needed

2 garlic cloves, crushed

2 tsp za'atar

Kosher salt

1 cup [240 ml] water

4 Tbsp [60 ml] extra-virgin olive oil

3 Tbsp tahini

1 Tbsp pine nuts, toasted (see page 81)

1 tsp chopped parsley

Place the chickpeas, lemon juice, garlic, za'atar, and 1½ tsp salt in the bowl of a food processor. Pulse to combine, then scrape down the sides of the bowl. Add ½ cup [120 ml] of the water, 2 Tbsp of the olive oil, and the tahini. Process until the mixture is creamy, adding up to ½ cup [120 ml] of the remaining water, 2 Tbsp at a time, processing after each addition until the mixture is the consistency you like. Taste, adding more lemon juice and salt if desired.

Store in an airtight container in the refrigerator for up to 2 weeks. Spoon the hummus into a serving bowl and top with the remaining 2 Tbsp olive oil, the toasted pine nuts, and parsley.

SPICY GUACAMOLE

I am "guac" obsessed, as apparently are the rest of my friends. I strive to find the perfect balance between adding enough ingredients to guacamole to be interesting without detracting from the star itself. This version earned a perfect 10. Lucky for all of us, avocados are considered one of nature's gifts to wellness; they're chock-full of potassium and vitamins B, C, and E, and an avocado has half of the recommended daily amount of fiber. My trick to keeping guacamole partially chunky yet a little smooth? I use a potato masher, a pastry cutter, or a molcajete (a traditional Mexican mortar and pestle), which allows you to mash until you reach the texture you like.

If you're sensitive to corn or tomatoes, you can simply omit them and substitute something else for crunch and texture, such as toasted pumpkin seeds or diced jicama. Also, plantain chips (see page 98) are a wonderful treat, but sliced jicama is another great choice to serve with the guacamole.

PREPARATION TIME
30 minutes

MAKES
2 cups / 480 g

---

4 ripe avocados, halved and pitted

Kosher salt

3 Tbsp lime juice

½ cup [90 g] fresh corn kernels from the cob (optional), toasted unsalted pumpkin seeds, or diced jicama

2 Tbsp minced red onion

1 Tbsp minced jalapeño, seeds removed (optional if nightshade-sensitive)

½ cup [100 g] chopped tomato (optional if nightshade-sensitive) or diced jicama

2 Tbsp chopped cilantro

2 to 3 dashes of hot sauce

Freshly ground black pepper

Place the avocados and a sprinkling of salt in a small bowl or molcajete. Mash until the desired consistency is reached, then stir in the lime juice.

Add the corn (if using), onion, and jalapeño (if using). Stir to combine. Gently mix in the tomato (if using) and cilantro. Taste, adding the hot sauce, a grinding of pepper, and more salt until the guacamole is well balanced and spicy enough for you.

Store, covered tightly with a layer of plastic wrap pressed onto the surface of guacamole to preserve freshness and slow oxidation, in the refrigerator for up to 2 days.

how salt helps

The kosher salt acts as an abrasive, keeping the avocados from slipping and sliding too much while you mash them.

TOMATILLO AND JALAPEÑO SALSA VERDE

In a quest to develop healthier snacks, I've often turned to ingredients used in Mexican food. This salsa is an example. I like the smoke imparted on the veggies when I grill them, but if you don't feel like grilling, you can broil them in the oven. This salsa also becomes the base for my Chicken Chile Verde (page 156). Note: If you are sensitive to nightshades, skip this recipe and opt for my chimichurri (see page 56) or pesto (see page 55) instead.

PREPARATION TIME
30 minutes

COOKING TIME
10 minutes

MAKES
3 cups / 690 g

1¼ lb [570 g] tomatillos, skins removed and rinsed

1 white onion, quartered through the root end and outer skin removed

2 jalapeños, halved lengthwise

2 Tbsp extra-virgin olive oil

Kosher salt

3 Tbsp lime juice, plus more as needed

2 Tbsp chopped cilantro

Prepare a grill for cooking over medium-high heat.

Place the tomatillos, onion, and jalapeños in a large bowl and add the olive oil and ½ tsp salt. Toss to coat evenly, then place in a grilling basket or directly on the grill grates if they are narrowly spaced enough. Grill, turning the vegetables occasionally, until they begin to lightly char and soften, 5 to 10 minutes. Remove the vegetables from the grill as they are ready. (Alternatively, place an oven rack in the top third of an oven and preheat to broil. Transfer the vegetables to a foil-lined baking sheet. Broil the vegetables, watching closely and turning occasionally, until they are lightly charred and softened, 10 to 15 minutes.) Transfer to the same bowl to catch their juices and let cool to room temperature.

Place the cooled vegetables along with their juices in a blender and add the lime juice, cilantro, and another pinch of salt. Blend on low speed or pulse until the mixture reaches the texture of a salsa. Taste, adding more salt or lime juice as desired.

Store in an airtight container in the refrigerator for up to 5 days.

CURRIED DEVILED EGGS

Deviled eggs can be a nutritious snack or appetizer. The addition of curry powder adds an anti-inflammatory boost while providing fantastic flavor. Finely grating the egg yolks before mixing them with the mayonnaise helps achieve a silky-smooth texture and decreases the need for so much mayonnaise. Cutting the eggs crosswise is a fun, modern way to serve them.

PREPARATION TIME
20 minutes

COOKING TIME
12 minutes

SERVES
6

6 eggs

1 small shallot, finely chopped

3 Tbsp mayonnaise or Vegenaise

½ tsp Dijon mustard

1 tsp lemon juice, plus more as needed

2 tsp curry powder

Kosher salt

Pinch of cayenne pepper

1 Tbsp finely chopped cilantro

Place the eggs in a medium saucepan and cover with water by 1 in [2.5 cm]. Bring to a rapid boil. Remove from the heat, cover, and let stand for 12 minutes. Fill a medium bowl with ice water. Transfer the eggs to the ice-water bath and let stand for 10 minutes.

Meanwhile, in a medium bowl, whisk together the shallot, mayonnaise, mustard, lemon juice, curry powder, ⅛ tsp salt, cayenne, and 2 tsp of the cilantro. Set aside.

Crack each egg and carefully remove the shell. Using a very sharp knife, cut a very thin portion off the top and bottom of the egg to create flat surfaces, then halve each egg crosswise. Carefully remove the yolks from the whites, then place the whites, flat-side down, on a serving platter.

CONTINUED

Using a Microplane or a box grater, finely grate the egg yolks and add to the mayonnaise mixture. Stir until well combined and adjust the lemon juice and salt as desired.

Transfer the mayonnaise mixture to a pastry bag with a star tip and pipe into the egg whites. Garnish with the remaining 1 tsp cilantro.

Store in a covered container in the refrigerator for up to 8 hours.

makeshift pastry bag

If you don't have a pastry bag, create your own by transferring the mayonnaise mixture to a sealable plastic freezer bag and cutting off a corner. Alternatively, you can spoon the filling into the egg whites.

SPINACH AND ARTICHOKE DIP
with goat cheese

My friend and fellow cook Amanda Frederickson is always looking for alternatives to gluten and dairy in her cooking. We both do better with goat's milk than cow's milk, so she took on the challenge of finding an alternative to the sour cream and cream cheese typically used in spinach and artichoke dip. If you can't find goat's-milk cheddar you can replace it with traditional cow's-milk cheddar if you are not sensitive to lactose.

PREPARATION TIME
20 minutes

COOKING TIME
20–25 minutes

SERVES
6–8

---

1 Tbsp olive oil

1 yellow onion, finely chopped

2 garlic cloves, minced

One 14-oz [400-g] can artichoke hearts

One 16-oz [454-g] package frozen chopped spinach, defrosted, excess liquid squeezed out

1 cup [280 g] goat cheese

1½ cups [120 g] shredded goat's-milk cheddar

3 Tbsp mayonnaise or Vegenaise

2 tsp lemon juice

Kosher salt

Freshly ground black pepper

¼ tsp smoked paprika

Pinch of crushed red pepper flakes

Gluten-free pita wedges or fresh vegetables for serving

Preheat the oven to 350°F [180°C]. Lightly coat an 8-by-8-in [20-by-20-cm] baking dish with nonstick cooking spray.

In a medium sauté pan over medium heat, warm the olive oil. Add the onion and cook, stirring occasionally, until translucent, 4 to 5 minutes. Add the garlic and cook for 1 minute more. Remove the pan from the heat and set aside.

In the bowl of a food processor, combine the artichoke hearts, spinach, goat cheese, 1 cup [80 g] of the cheddar, the mayonnaise, lemon juice, 1 tsp salt, $1/4$ tsp black pepper, smoked paprika, and red pepper flakes. Process until smooth. Add the cooled onion mixture and pulse a few times to combine. Season with additional salt and pepper, if desired.

Transfer the mixture to the prepared baking dish. Sprinkle with the remaining $1/2$ cup [40 g] cheddar. Bake until heated through and the cheese on top is golden, 15 to 20 minutes.

Store in an airtight container in the refrigerator for up to 3 days. Bring to room temperature before serving with the pita wedges.

MARCONA ALMOND-STUFFED DATES
with orange zest

These sweet dates stuffed with salty Marcona almonds, then sautéed and finished with sea salt and orange zest, are strangely addictive. I dare you to eat just one.

PREPARATION TIME
15 minutes

COOKING TIME
2 minutes

SERVES
4–6

20 Medjool dates

20 to 40 Marcona almonds

2 Tbsp extra-virgin olive oil

2 tsp grated orange zest

½ tsp fleur de sel

Remove the pits from the dates. Gently stuff each date with 1 or 2 almonds, depending on the size of the date. Seal the almond inside by pressing the date around it.

In a medium sauté pan over medium heat, heat the olive oil. Add the dates and gently sauté until warmed through, about 2 minutes. Remove from the heat and sprinkle with the orange zest and fleur de sel.

Store in an airtight container in the refrigerator up to 2 days.

to remove date pits

To remove the pits from the dates, hold the date so a long side is horizontal. With a paring knife, gently make a slit and slip out the pit.

CEVICHE
with mango and jalapeños

With this ceviche, the sweetness of the mango offsets the spice of the jalapeños. If you are sensitive to nightshades, leave out the jalapeños and tomatoes.

PREPARATION TIME	COOKING TIME	SERVES
40 minutes	30 minutes	6–10

1 lb [455 g] tilapia, diced into ½-in [12-mm] pieces

½ cup [120 ml] lime juice

Kosher salt

2 jalapeños, minced (optional if nightshade-sensitive)

¼ cup [35 g] finely diced red onion

2 Roma tomatoes, diced (optional if nightshade-sensitive)

1 mango, peeled, pitted, and diced

¼ cup [40 g] seeded and diced cucumber

2 Tbsp minced cilantro

2 avocados, halved, pitted, and diced

2 to 3 dashes of hot sauce

Freshly ground black pepper

Place the tilapia, lime juice, and 1 tsp salt in a shallow, nonreactive dish, such as ceramic or glass. Stir to coat the fish with the lime juice, then add the jalapeños (if using) and red onion. Cover and refrigerate for 30 minutes, allowing the citrus to cook the fish through. The fish will be opaque when ready.

Add the tomatoes (if using), mango, cucumber, and cilantro to the fish. Stir to combine. Gently fold in the avocado. Season with hot sauce, pepper, and additional salt. Serve immediately.

fish substitutions

Feel free to substitute red snapper, shrimp, or even sliced scallops for the tilapia. This recipe serves up to ten because it always goes so fast, but you can easily halve it.

chapter

4

VEGETABLES AND LEGUMES

Increasing the amount of vegetables in our diet is inarguably a great idea and is a key strategy for replacing problematic foods. From leafy greens to mushrooms loaded with vitamin B, there are so many vegetables that help fight inflammation. For this reason, I often make large batches of vegetable side dishes because everyone at my table wants seconds. I then can minimize the amount of red meat to side dish, proportionally. These recipes can also be served as main dishes. Whenever I make a batch of the broccoli, trumpet mushrooms, or sesame soba noodles, they definitely become the entrée.

VEGAN MINESTRONE
with Herb Oil

I love eating soup, but don't love making it, so I set out to make a soup that had enough ingredients to be delicious but was low maintenance enough that I wouldn't be chopping, slicing, and dicing all day. The result? A vegan—yes, vegan!—soup that is out of this world. Loaded with zucchini, chard, and tons of beans, this soup is a veggie lover's dream come true. The extra flavor boost comes from the herb oil, so try not to skip it. If you're sensitive to nightshades, omit the tomato paste and substitute vegetable stock for the canned tomatoes.

PREPARATION TIME
30 minutes

COOKING TIME
40 minutes

SERVES
8

3 Tbsp olive oil

1 cup [140 g] diced carrots

¾ cup [70 g] diced celery

1 yellow onion, sliced

Kosher salt

1 Tbsp tomato paste (optional if nightshade-sensitive)

2 garlic cloves, minced

Pinch of crushed red pepper flakes

4 zucchini, diced

2 crookneck squash, diced

8 cups [2 L] low-sodium vegetable broth

Two 14.5-oz [410-g] cans diced San Marzano tomatoes or 1 qt [960 ml] vegetable stock

1 bunch rainbow chard, stems removed, coarsely chopped

Two 15-oz [425-g] cans cannellini beans, rinsed and drained

HERB OIL

¼ tsp kosher salt

2 garlic cloves, peeled

½ cup [120 ml] extra-virgin olive oil

½ cup [20 g] packed herbs, such as parsley, chives, basil, and mint

In a large stockpot or Dutch oven over medium heat, warm the olive oil. Add the carrots, celery, onion, and ½ tsp salt and cook, stirring frequently, until tender, about 10 minutes. Add the tomato paste (if using), garlic, and red pepper flakes and cook until the paste turns brick red, about 1 minute. Add the zucchini and squash and cook for 1 minute. Stir in the broth and tomatoes, bring to a boil over high heat, then turn the heat to medium-low and simmer uncovered for 15 minutes. Stir in the chard and simmer for 5 minutes longer. Stir in the beans and warm them for about 3 minutes. Season with salt.

In the meantime, make the herb oil: Place the salt and garlic in a small food processor or blender and process until the garlic is minced, about 20 seconds. Add the olive oil and herbs and blend until the oil is bright green, about 20 seconds.

Fill each bowl with soup and drizzle with 2 tsp of the herb oil to serve.

SHAVED FENNEL AND CITRUS SALAD
with toasted pistachios

With its licorice flavor and solid crunch, fennel is delicious raw. A classic way to serve it is with citrus, some good extra-virgin olive oil, and a hefty shaving of Parmigiano-Reggiano. Adding mixed greens is a way to add texture. With grilled shrimp, it becomes an entrée.

PREPARATION TIME
25 minutes

SERVES
4

4 cups [120 g] mixed greens

½ cup [20 g] packed parsley leaves

1 fennel bulb, cored and thinly sliced

1 medium shallot, thinly sliced

¼ cup [35 g] pistachios, toasted (see page 81)

2 navel oranges, segmented, plus 2 Tbsp orange juice

1 Tbsp lemon juice

3 Tbsp extra-virgin olive oil

Kosher salt

Freshly ground black pepper

½ cup [20 g] shaved Parmigiano-Reggiano

Place the greens, parsley, fennel, shallot, pistachios, and orange segments in a large bowl.

In another large bowl, whisk together the 2 Tbsp orange juice, lemon juice, olive oil, ¼ tsp salt, and a grinding of pepper to form a vinaigrette. Drizzle ¼ cup [60 ml] of the vinaigrette over the salad, and toss to coat. Taste, adding more salt as desired. Sprinkle with the Parmigiano-Reggiano and toss gently. Serve, passing the remaining vinaigrette at the table.

how to segment oranges and other citrus

To segment an orange, cut off the ends and place a flat end on a cutting board. Using a sharp paring knife, cut the orange from top to bottom in sections to remove the skin and white pith. Turn and repeat. Working over a bowl, cut each orange segment from the membrane. The segments will fall into the bowl along with the juice.

GREEN PAPAYA SALAD

Many Southeast Asian recipes strive to balance four of the sensations of taste: sweet, sour, salty, and umami. In its classic Lao or Thai version, green papaya salad—known as *tam som* in Laos and *som tam* in Thailand—has all these characteristics; the unripe papaya is sour, the palm sugar is sweet, the dried shrimp is salty, and the tomatoes and fish sauce bring the umami. Green papaya aids digestion, soothes inflammation, and even helps battle nausea. For an update of the traditional salad, I replaced the peanuts with my favorite Marcona almonds. If you're sensitive to nightshades, omit the chiles and tomatoes.

PREPARATION TIME
30 minutes

COOKING TIME
5 minutes

SERVES
8

8 oz [230 g] green beans, trimmed

½ cup [120 ml] lime juice

3 Tbsp fish sauce

2 Tbsp agave nectar or brown sugar

2 red Thai chiles, seeded and thinly sliced (optional if nightshade-sensitive)

2 green papayas, each about 12 oz [340 g], peeled, seeded, and julienned

2 cups [330 g] cherry tomatoes, halved (optional if nightshade-sensitive)

½ cup [15 g] chopped cilantro

½ cup [15 g] chopped mint

½ cup [70 g] coarsely chopped Marcona almonds

Bring a pot of salted water to a boil and fill a medium bowl with ice water. Add the green beans to the boiling water and cook for 2 minutes. With a slotted spoon, transfer the beans to the ice-water bath to stop the cooking. Be careful not to overcook the beans; they should still have some bite. Dry the beans and slice in half crosswise.

In a small bowl, whisk together the lime juice, fish sauce, agave nectar, and chiles (if using) to make a dressing.

Place the green beans, papayas, tomatoes (if using), cilantro, and mint in a serving bowl. Add the dressing and toss to coat. Stir in half of the almonds, then sprinkle the rest on top and serve.

QUINOA SALAD
with radishes, currants, and mint

Since I omitted gluten from my diet, quinoa has become my be-all and end-all grain for salads and side dishes. This recipe is an iteration of a favorite couscous salad that I've managed to make more healthful. The currants lend sweetness, while the radishes add a little heat and the carrots give some crunch. Sometimes I add toasted pine nuts or cashews. Taking an extra five minutes to slice the veggies neatly creates a showstopper of a recipe.

PREPARATION TIME
20 minutes

SERVES
4–6

6 cups [850 g] cooked rainbow, white, or red quinoa, cooled (see page 67)

½ cup [120 ml] Garlic-Lemon Vinaigrette (page 52)

½ cup [80 g] currants

½ cup [50 g] thinly sliced green onions, white and light green parts only

5 radishes, thinly sliced

2 carrots, peeled and cut into ¼-in [6-mm] matchsticks

3 Tbsp finely chopped mint

1 Tbsp lemon juice

½ cup [70 g] toasted pine nuts or cashews

Kosher salt

Freshly ground black pepper

Combine the quinoa with ⅓ cup [80 ml] of the vinaigrette in a large bowl. Add the currants, green onions, radishes, carrots, mint, lemon juice, and pine nuts and mix gently with a spoon. Taste, adding up to ½ tsp salt and a fresh grinding of pepper.

The salad can be held at room temperature for up to 6 hours. Before serving, stir in the remaining vinaigrette.

CHOPPED KALE SALAD
with quinoa and Garlic-Lemon Vinaigrette

Kale is now a commonplace green. Unlike lettuces, it benefits from a long soak in vinaigrette, which softens the leaves without making them soggy. Also, cutting the kale into thin ribbons transforms the texture from a mouthful to toothsome. I like the combination of the currants with the pine nuts here. Feel free to use the kale and vinaigrette as a base for different seasonal salads, such as fresh corn and tomatoes in summer or roasted butternut squash and cranberries in fall.

PREPARATION TIME
20 minutes

SERVES
4 as a side dish / 2 as a main dish

---

1 bunch lacinato kale leaves, thinly sliced

¼ cup [60 ml] Garlic-Lemon Vinaigrette (page 52)

½ cup [100 g] cooked quinoa (see page 67)

¼ cup [30 g] thinly sliced red onion

3 Tbsp currants

3 Tbsp pine nuts, toasted (see page 81)

2 Tbsp grated Parmigiano-Reggiano (optional)

Place the kale in a large bowl. Toss with the vinaigrette and let it sit for at least 30 minutes at room temperature, or up to 4 hours in the refrigerator. Add the quinoa, onion, currants, pine nuts, and Parmigiano-Reggiano (if using). Toss, breaking up any clumps of quinoa so it's evenly distributed throughout the salad. Serve immediately.

the best way to cut kale

Chiffonade is a fancy term for "thinly sliced." I like the taste of kale when I cut it into a chiffonade. To do so, stack three kale leaves, then roll them up tightly lengthwise. Cut the leaves crosswise into ¼-in [6-mm] slices. Use in salads, for sautéing, smoothies, and any other recipe that calls for kale.

FRENCH LENTIL SALAD
with roasted cauliflower and herbs

As I've started to limit the amount of animal fats in my diet, lentils have become a more significant staple in my kitchen. They're versatile and filling and make a great base for building flavors. Lentilles du Puy are a green variety from the Auvergne region of France. They are a bit more expensive than other lentils, but they're worth it because they have a little less starch than the standard variety so they hold their texture and don't turn mushy. If you're sensitive to nightshades, leave out the tomatoes.

PREPARATION TIME
30 minutes

COOKING TIME
25–30 minutes

SERVES
6–8

2 cups [670 g] cauliflower florets

2 Tbsp extra-virgin olive oil

Kosher salt

1 tsp fennel seeds (optional)

1 tsp lemon juice or to taste

1½ cups [300 g] French green lentils

1 qt [960 ml] water or vegetable broth

French Vinaigrette (page 50)

1 small carrot, peeled and diced

½ cup [60 g] thinly sliced red onion

½ cup [100 g] quartered cherry tomatoes (optional if nightshade-sensitive)

½ cup [90 g] dried cherries

2 Tbsp chopped mint

1 Tbsp chopped chives

1 Tbsp chopped parsley

Freshly ground black pepper

CONTINUED

Preheat the oven to 450°F [230°C]. Use the convection setting if available.

Place the cauliflower in a large bowl. Coat with the olive oil and season with a generous pinch of salt and the fennel seeds (if using). Stir in the lemon juice. Spread the cauliflower evenly on a baking sheet. Roast for 10 minutes. Remove from the oven and stir, then roast until the cauliflower has caramelized and is just cooked through, 5 to 10 minutes.

Spread the lentils on a separate baking sheet and remove any small stones or misshapen pieces. Transfer the lentils to a strainer and rinse. Place the lentils in a pot along with the water. Bring to a boil, lower the heat, and simmer partially covered until the lentils are just cooked through, 25 to 30 minutes. They should be tender but have the slightest bite. Drain the excess water.

Place the warm lentils in a large bowl and toss with half of the vinaigrette. Add the cauliflower, carrot, onion, tomatoes (if using), dried cherries, and herbs. Gently stir to combine, adding more vinaigrette if needed. Season with salt and pepper.

The salad can be held in the refrigerator for up to 3 days. Let come to room temperature before serving.

RED LENTIL CURRY

with cauliflower and yams

I tend to become a creature of habit and, in a pinch, use the same herbs and spices in my food night after night. Basil, rosemary, thyme, repeat. However, cooks from countries such as Thailand and India are pros at incorporating the most powerful anti-inflammatory spices and herbs in their everyday cooking, so I follow their lead in my quest to feel better. Now curry spice blends, garam masala, and a variety of spices are always in my pantry. If you are sensitive to nightshades, consider leaving out the curry paste.

PREPARATION TIME
30 minutes

COOKING TIME
45 minutes

SERVES
4–6

---

2 Tbsp organic canola oil

1 yellow onion, diced

2 tsp grated fresh ginger

2 garlic cloves, minced

1 Tbsp red curry paste (optional if nightshade-sensitive)

1 tsp garam masala

Kosher salt

Freshly ground black pepper

4 cups [960 ml] water

One 14-oz [400-ml] can unsweetened coconut milk

2 Tbsp lime juice

1 Tbsp agave nectar

1½ cups [280 g] red lentils

2 small garnet yams, diced

1 small head cauliflower, cut into small florets

Steamed brown rice for serving (optional)

Cilantro for garnish

In a Dutch oven or large stockpot over medium heat, warm the canola oil. Add the onion and cook, stirring frequently, until soft, 8 to 10 minutes. Turn the heat to low and add the ginger and garlic. Cook, stirring frequently, until fragrant, about 1 minute. Add the curry paste (if using), garam masala, 1 tsp salt, and $1/2$ tsp pepper and cook, stirring frequently, for 1 minute.

Add the water, turn the heat to medium-high, and bring to a boil, scraping up the browned bits on the bottom of the pot. Add the coconut milk, lime juice, agave nectar, and lentils and bring to a boil. Cover, turn the heat to medium-low, and simmer for 10 minutes.

Add the yams and cauliflower to the pot, cover, and simmer until the lentils are cooked through, about 15 minutes. Season with salt and pepper. Serve over steamed brown rice, if desired, and garnish with cilantro.

THAI RED CURRY

with tofu and green beans

Curries, loaded with the right spices, ginger, and chiles, are an anti-inflammatory go-to. This version is so flexible that it works with tofu, chicken, hearty white fish, mussels, or scallops. Blanching the green beans is not required unless you like them to be vibrant green, as I do. If you skip the blanching, add the beans with the tofu. The chile and curry paste in this recipe are important to its flavor, but if you are sensitive to nightshades, omit the chile and cherry tomatoes and cut the curry paste in half.

PREPARATION TIME	COOKING TIME	SERVES
35 minutes	25 minutes	6–8

---

8 oz [230 g] green beans, trimmed and cut into 1-in [2.5-cm] pieces

1 Tbsp organic canola oil

1 large red onion, sliced

Kosher salt

1½ tsp minced garlic

1 tsp minced fresh ginger

1 Thai bird chile or small serrano chile, very thinly sliced (optional if nightshade-sensitive)

4 Tbsp [60 g] Thai red curry paste (2 Tbsp if nightshade-sensitive)

Two 14-oz [400-ml] cans unsweetened coconut milk

1 cup [240 ml] chicken or vegetable stock

⅓ cup [80 ml] lime juice

¼ cup [60 ml] fish sauce, plus more as needed

3 Tbsp honey

2 lb [910 g] extra-firm tofu, cut into 1-in [2.5-cm] cubes

1½ cups [230 g] cherry tomatoes, halved (optional if nightshade-sensitive)

¼ cup [10 g] chopped basil

1 lb [455 g] dried brown rice noodles, such as Annie Chun's Pad Thai Brown Rice Noodles

CONTINUED

Bring a pot of salted water to a boil and fill a medium bowl with ice water. Add the green beans to the boiling water and cook for 2 minutes. With a slotted spoon, transfer the beans to the ice-water bath to stop the cooking. Be careful not to overcook the beans, they should still have some bite. Dry the beans.

In a large stockpot or Dutch oven over medium heat, warm the canola oil. Add the onion and a pinch of salt and cook, stirring occasionally, until softened, 6 to 8 minutes. Add the garlic, ginger, chile (if using), and curry paste and cook, stirring, until fragrant, about 1 minute. Add the coconut milk, chicken stock, lime juice, fish sauce, and honey and bring to a boil. Turn the heat to medium-low and simmer, uncovered, to combine the flavors, about 10 minutes.

Turn the heat to medium-high, add the tofu, and simmer, stirring occasionally, for 3 minutes. Add the tomatoes (if using) and blanched green beans. Continue to simmer until the tofu is warmed through, the green beans are crisp-tender, and the sauce has thickened slightly, about 2 minutes. Stir in the basil. Taste and add more fish sauce or salt as desired.

Prepare the rice noodles according to the package instructions. Place a serving of noodles in the bottom of each bowl and top with a few ladlesful of the curry. Serve immediately.

about curry paste

Curry paste and fish sauce can vary drastically in quality. If you are fortunate enough to have an Asian market nearby, ask for recommendations, and if you are using an unfamiliar brand, always taste the product on its own before adding to your dish. When shopping at a typical grocery store, I look for the Thai Kitchen brand of fish sauce and red curry paste.

SESAME SOBA
with asparagus and mushrooms

Buckwheat is the seed of a broadleaf plant that can be cooked whole or ground and used like flour. Soba made with buckwheat is an excellent gluten-free alternative to wheat pastas and rice noodles, which lack nutritional value. Because buckwheat stabilizes blood sugar, lowers cholesterol, and fights inflammation, it is classified as a superfood. If you're looking to live without gluten, make sure your soba noodles have not been produced on the same equipment as wheat-based products and are totally gluten-free.

PREPARATION TIME
25 minutes

COOKING TIME
25 minutes

SERVES
4

One 9.5-oz [269-g] package buckwheat soba noodles

3 Tbsp toasted sesame oil

2 Tbsp tamari, plus more as needed

1 Tbsp lime juice, plus more as needed

2 tsp honey

2 Tbsp sesame seeds

4 cups [280 g] sliced King Trumpet or shiitake mushrooms

Kosher salt

2 cups [220 g] sliced asparagus

1 carrot, peeled and julienned

2 garlic cloves, minced

2 Tbsp chopped mint

2 Tbsp chopped basil

2 green onions, white and light green parts only, thinly sliced

Prepare the soba noodles according to the package instructions. While they're cooking, whisk together 2 Tbsp of the sesame oil, the tamari, lime juice, and honey. When the noodles are done, drain them, rinse with cool water, then place in a medium bowl and toss with the tamari mixture.

CONTINUED

Place a cast-iron or nonstick skillet over medium-high heat. Add the sesame seeds and toast, stirring constantly, until fragrant and just browned, about 2 minutes. Add to the noodles.

Return the pan to medium-high heat. When it is very hot, add 2 tsp of the remaining sesame oil and swirl, then add the mushrooms and a pinch of salt. Allow the mushrooms to sit without stirring until seared on one side, about 2 minutes, then stir and cook for 2 minutes more. Place the mushrooms in a small bowl to cool.

Add the remaining 1 tsp sesame oil to the pan, followed by the asparagus. Cook for 1 minute, then add the carrot, garlic, and a pinch of salt and cook for 2 minutes. Add the vegetables to the mushrooms and allow to cool a bit, then place in the bowl with the noodles. Toss with the herbs and green onions. Taste, adding additional lime juice or tamari if needed for balance. Serve immediately.

PAN-SEARED MUSHROOMS
with caramelized shallots and thyme

Mushrooms are the new steak. Well, maybe not truly, but they are so meaty and filling that I eat them often as an entrée. When you look to add more foods to your diet that reduce inflammation, this recipe is a standout. Fresh cultivated mushrooms like King Trumpets and shiitakes are full of zinc, iron, potassium, calcium, phosphorus, vitamin C, folic acid, niacin, and vitamins B-1 and B-2. I top mushrooms with a poached egg (see page 71) for breakfast or serve them alongside kale salad (see page 126) for dinner.

PREPARATION TIME
15 minutes

COOKING TIME
6–10 minutes

SERVES
2

2 Tbsp extra-virgin olive oil

4 cups [280 g] sliced mushrooms, such as King Trumpet, shiitake, and cremini

Kosher or sea salt

2 Tbsp minced shallots

1 Tbsp lemon juice

2 tsp thyme leaves

Freshly ground black pepper

In a large nonstick skillet over medium-high heat, warm 1 Tbsp of the olive oil. When it smokes, add the mushrooms and a generous pinch of salt. Sear the mushrooms until they are browned on one side and begin to release some of their liquid, about 1 minute. Stir to move the uncooked mushrooms to the bottom of the pan.

Cook until the mushrooms have released their liquid and it has mostly evaporated, 3 to 4 minutes. Add the shallots and cook for 1 minute. Stir in the lemon juice and thyme. Allow the lemon juice to evaporate, about 30 seconds.

Remove the pan from the heat and add the remaining 1 Tbsp olive oil. Finish with another sprinkling of salt and a grinding of pepper. Serve immediately.

CRISPY OVEN-ROASTED BROCCOLI
with Italian Spice Trio

Roasted in high heat, broccoli caramelizes and winds up crispy and sweet. Loaded with B vitamins, vitamin K, and omega-3 fatty acids, it has significant anti-inflammatory properties. For extra health benefits, I toss the roasted broccoli in olive oil and a simple spice blend (good on any vegetable or sprinkled on chicken or fish before grilling). I then finish with a generous squeeze of lemon. It's a total crowd-pleaser.

PREPARATION TIME
15 minutes

COOKING TIME
15–20 minutes

SERVES
4

ITALIAN SPICE TRIO

2 Tbsp dried oregano

2 Tbsp fennel seeds

½ tsp crushed red pepper flakes

1 large or 2 small heads broccoli, cut into 1-in [2.5-cm] florets

¼ cup [60 ml] extra-virgin olive oil

1 tsp kosher salt

¼ tsp freshly ground black pepper

Zest and juice of 1 lemon

To make the spice trio: Combine the oregano, fennel seeds, and red pepper flakes in an airtight container. Store at room temperature for up to 1 month.

Place two racks in the lower third of the oven and preheat the oven to 450°F [230°C]. Use the convection setting if available.

Combine the broccoli, olive oil, 1 Tbsp of the spice trio, salt, pepper, and lemon zest in a large bowl. Stir to coat the broccoli evenly. Spread the broccoli evenly on two baking sheets. Roast for 10 minutes. Remove from the oven and stir. Place the sheets on opposite racks and roast until the broccoli has caramelized and is just cooked through, 5 to 10 minutes. Stir in 1 tsp lemon juice, adding more to taste. Serve hot or at room temperature.

chapter

5

FISH, CHICKEN, PORK, LAMB, AND BEEF

Over the past few decades, numerous factors have changed our dinner habits. The average size of a dinner plate has increased by 30 percent, encouraging us to eat 20 percent more every night. Forty years ago, we consumed 2,169 calories a day, and today we consume 2,642 a day, a 23 percent increase. In addition, anxiety and stress have increased, causing many of us to eat more and consume more alcohol. With all these barriers to good health, how can we manage to eat well-balanced, inflammation-fighting dinners? One way is removing the obstacles to cooking. Dinner recipes have to be approachable, fairly quick, and healthful.

Proteins, still an important part of our diet, have certain health benefits that other foods do not provide with the same potency. Salmon and grass-fed beef supply us with omega-3 fatty acids, promoting heart health and counterbalancing mood disorders and autoimmune diseases. Chicken continues to be a fantastic source of lean protein. It's all about finding the right balance between the amount of meat I have on the plate along with the vegetables.

GRILLED CHIPOTLE SHRIMP SKEWERS

I like using chipotles in adobo to add depth of flavor to grilled foods. Balanced with lime and honey, they make the perfect marinade for grilled shrimp, chicken, or any type of white fish. If you are sensitive to nightshades, omit the chipotles and let the ancho chile powder do the work. Serve with black beans (see page 66) or kale salad (see page 126), subbing Chipotle-Lime Vinaigrette (page 54) for the regular version. The marinade yields 1 cup [240 ml], enough for 3 lb [1.4 kg] of protein, so if you have some left over, it can be frozen or stored in the refrigerator for up to one week.

PREPARATION TIME
35 minutes
(plus 2–12 hours to marinate)

COOKING TIME
15 minutes

SERVES
4

½ cup [120 ml] organic canola oil

¼ cup [60 ml] lime juice

2 to 3 Tbsp chipotles in adobo (optional if nightshade-sensitive)

1 Tbsp honey

¼ red onion, coarsely chopped

2 garlic cloves, coarsely chopped

2 to 3 tsp hot sauce

2 tsp ancho chile powder

1 tsp ground cumin

1 tsp dried oregano

1 tsp kosher salt

½ tsp freshly ground black pepper

1½ lb [680 g] shrimp, peeled and deveined, tails on

Place the canola oil, lime juice, 2 Tbsp of the chipotles in adobo, honey, onion, garlic, 2 tsp of the hot sauce, chile powder, cumin, oregano, salt, and pepper in a blender or food processor. Puree until smooth to make a marinade. Taste and adjust with more chipotle or hot sauce as desired.

Place the shrimp in a nonreactive dish, such as ceramic or glass, or in a sealable plastic bag. Pour half of the marinade over the shrimp. Toss the shrimp to evenly coat. Cover and refrigerate for 2 hours, or up to 12 hours.

Prepare a grill for cooking over medium-high heat. Alternatively, preheat a grill pan over medium-high heat. When the grill or pan is hot, use a folded paper towel to lightly oil the grill rack or pan. Soak eight 9-in [23-cm] bamboo skewers in water for at least 30 minutes before cooking.

Thread the shrimp onto the skewers, allowing the marinade to drip off over the bowl, and set on a baking sheet (to transport the skewers to the grill).

Place the shrimp skewers on the grill or grill pan and cook until they are just pink and opaque, about 2 minutes per side. Serve warm or at room temperature.

SALADE NIÇOISE
with salmon and beets

The city of Nice on the French Riviera is known for this luscious salad with local oil-cured olives, oil-packed tuna, and anchovies—three foods with huge health benefits. When I don't have access to quality tuna or anchovies, I replace them with fresh salmon. For added health benefits, I substitute roasted baby beets for the starchy potatoes. Because this is a composed salad, it has a few parts that need to be completed. Doing them all at once is too much for a weeknight. My solution? I hard-boil eggs, roast beets, and make vinaigrette on the weekend, then use them during the week for this salad and other recipes.

PREPARATION TIME
30 minutes

COOKING TIME
20 minutes

SERVES
4

2 baby beets, peeled and cut into large dice

2 Tbsp extra-virgin olive oil

8 oz [230 g] green beans, trimmed

Four 4-oz [115-g] skin-on salmon fillets, pin bones removed

Kosher salt

French Vinaigrette (page 50)

Freshly ground black pepper

1 cup [180 g] halved cherry tomatoes (optional if nightshade-sensitive)

3 hard-boiled eggs, quartered

½ cup [70 g] oil-cured Niçoise olives, pitted

1 Tbsp minced chives

Preheat the oven to 400°F [200°C].

In a small roasting pan, toss the beets with 1 Tbsp of the olive oil. Roast, stirring every 10 to 15 minutes, until the beets are soft and caramelized, about 40 minutes. Set aside to cool.

Bring a pot of salted water to a boil and fill a medium bowl with ice water. Add the green beans to the boiling water and cook for 2 minutes. With a slotted spoon, transfer the beans to the ice-water bath to stop the cooking. Be careful not to overcook the beans, they should still have some bite. Dry the beans.

Rinse the salmon and pat dry with a paper towel. Sprinkle each side with a small pinch of salt.

Place a medium nonstick sauté pan over medium-high heat. When the pan is hot, add the remaining 1 Tbsp olive oil. Place the salmon fillets skin-side down in the pan and cook until the skin is crispy, about 2 minutes. For medium-rare salmon, turn the fillets and cook for 1 minute more. For medium salmon, also turn the salmon on its sides, cooking each side for 1 minute. Remove and place on a wire rack so the skin doesn't get soggy.

Place the green beans in a medium bowl, add 1 Tbsp of the vinaigrette, and toss to coat. Taste and add a pinch of salt and pepper if needed. Arrange the beans in a pile on a serving platter. Repeat with the beets and cherry tomatoes (if using). Add the hard-boiled eggs and olives to the platter, then top with the salmon fillets. Drizzle with a little vinaigrette, then sprinkle with the chives. Serve family style.

HONEY MUSTARD–GLAZED SALMON

This recipe is unapologetically easy to make yet is a complete hit with both kids and adults every time I serve it. Although I'm a year-round griller, the recipe also works beautifully in the oven. You'll notice that I cook the salmon with the skin on and then remove it. Why? Cooking it with the skin on retains a lot of the moisture in the fish.

PREPARATION TIME
15 minutes

COOKING TIME
8 minutes

SERVES
4

4 Tbsp [90 g] honey

2 Tbsp Dijon mustard

Four 4-oz [115-g] skin-on salmon fillets, about 1 in [2.5 cm] thick, pin bones removed

Olive oil for brushing

Kosher salt

Freshly ground black pepper

In a small bowl, whisk together the honey and mustard. Set aside.

Rinse the salmon and pat dry with a paper towel. Brush all sides of each fillet with olive oil and season with a pinch each of salt and pepper.

To grill the salmon, prepare a grill for direct cooking over medium-high heat. Fold a 24-by-12-in [62-by-31-cm] piece of aluminum foil to create a square. Crimp the edges upward to form a rim. Prick the foil several times with a fork, then brush with olive oil.

Place the foil directly on the grill grate, then set the salmon, skin-side down, on the foil, leaving 1 in [2.5 cm] between each piece. Close the lid and grill for 4 minutes. Lift the lid and generously brush the fish with the honey mustard. Close the lid and grill for 2 to 3 minutes more for medium, or until the salmon is cooked to the desired doneness. Remove the salmon from the grill.

To cook the salmon in the oven, place a rack in the top third of the oven and preheat the oven to broil. Line a baking sheet with aluminum foil and brush with olive oil. Place the salmon, skin-side down, on the foil, leaving 1 in [2.5 cm] between each piece. Broil for 2 minutes, then liberally brush each fillet with the honey mustard. Continue broiling for 3 to 4 minutes more, or until the salmon is cooked to the desired doneness. Remove the salmon from the oven.

Brush the salmon with more honey mustard and let rest for 3 to 5 minutes before serving.

easy salmon skin removal

You'll notice that the salmon skin sticks to the foil, allowing the flesh to slide right off. If you like to eat the skin, you can peel it off, roll it up, and serve it alongside the fish.

SEARED AHI TUNA
with Peperonata

At its price, ahi tuna is a special-occasion food in my house. I like to serve it with something so tasty that people still feel satisfied with just a 4-oz [115-g] portion. The peperonata is substantive and tasty. Together, the pairing offers an abundance of healthful Mediterranean flavors.

PREPARATION TIME
15 minutes

COOKING TIME
60 minutes

SERVES
4

One 1-lb [455-g] ahi tuna fillet, about 1 in [2.5 cm] thick

Extra-virgin olive oil for brushing

Kosher salt

Freshly ground black pepper

1 cup [210 g] Peperonata (page 60)

Prepare a grill for direct cooking over high heat.

Brush the tuna fillet with olive oil and season with salt and pepper. Sear the tuna for 1 to 2 minutes per side for rare, or longer to reach the desired doneness. Transfer to a carving board and let rest for 2 minutes.

Slice the tuna against the grain and divide among four plates. Spoon one-fourth of the peperonata over each piece of fish and serve.

how to buy tuna

My trick to buying good tuna? I *always* ask the fishmonger to pull a piece from the back for me, not from the display case even if the tuna is right in front of me. The fishmonger should be able to tell you when it came in and should also be happy to cut off a piece from a large, fresh fish.

FISH EN PAPILLOTE
with tomatoes, corn, and asparagus

Cooking fish in parchment packets seals in moisture while creating a beautiful presentation with loads of flavor. Learn this technique and use it over and over again with any type of fish and your favorite seasonal vegetables.

PREPARATION TIME
30 minutes

COOKING TIME
20 minutes

SERVES
4

Four 4-oz [115-g] fish fillets, such as halibut, salmon, or snapper, pin bones removed

Kosher salt

Freshly ground black pepper

Extra-virgin olive oil for drizzling

2 lemons, preferably Meyer, ends trimmed, cut into 12 slices about ⅛ in [3 mm] thick

Kernels from 2 ears of corn

16 asparagus spears, bottoms trimmed, sliced on the bias into ½-in [12-mm] pieces

1 cup [160 g] cherry tomatoes (optional if nightshade-sensitive)

2 Tbsp finely chopped assorted herbs, such as basil, chives, parsley, tarragon, and dill

---

Preheat the oven to 400°F [200°C]. Cut four pieces of parchment paper each 18 in [46 cm] long.

Place a fish fillet on the center of a piece of parchment. Season with a small pinch each of salt and pepper, then drizzle with olive oil. Place three lemon slices on the fillet, overlapping them slightly to cover the fish. Sprinkle one-fourth each of the corn, asparagus, and tomatoes (if using) evenly around the fish, then drizzle with a little olive oil and season again with a small pinch each of salt and pepper.

Bring the long sides of the paper together, and fold the top edges down together to create a 1-in [2.5-cm] seal, then continue to fold down tightly over the fish and vegetables. Twist the open ends of the parchment in opposite directions to prevent steam from escaping.

CONTINUED

Repeat the process with the remaining ingredients and parchment. Place the packets on a baking sheet. (If not baking immediately, refrigerate for up to 4 hours.)

Bake until the packets are lightly browned and have puffed up, about 15 minutes. Transfer each packet to a plate and let stand for 5 minutes. Using sharp scissors, cut an X into the center of each packet and carefully pull back the parchment and sprinkle with the herbs. Serve immediately.

CRISPY FISH TACOS
with Mango Salsa

Fish tacos are one of my signature dishes, so I decided to do a greatest-hits recipe that combines favorite elements: avocado crema, sweet and spicy mango salsa, and sautéed tilapia. If you like crunch, the gluten-free flour and grated Parmesan is a much better alternative to the standard coating for frying the fish, without any sacrifice of flavor. You can make these more healthful by simply sprinkling the fish with chili powder and salt before sautéing or grilling it. Because corn is a trigger food for me, I simply wrap my fish in lettuce like many do for burgers (or I substitute the corn tortillas for a good-quality gluten- and corn-free version, such as the ones from Rudi's). If you are sensitive to nightshades, don't add the jalapeño to your salsa.

PREPARATION TIME
30 minutes

COOKING TIME
10 minutes

SERVES
4

MANGO SALSA

2 mangoes, peeled, pitted, and diced

½ small red onion, finely diced

1 jalapeño, minced (optional if nightshade-sensitive)

2 Tbsp lime juice, plus more as needed

2 Tbsp finely chopped cilantro

Kosher salt

AVOCADO CREMA

2 avocados, halved and pitted

Kosher salt

2 Tbsp mayonnaise or Vegenaise

2 Tbsp lime juice, plus more as needed

CONTINUED

1 lb [455 g] tilapia fillets or other white-fleshed fish, such as snapper

Kosher salt

Freshly ground black pepper

2 eggs

1 cup [140 g] Cup4Cup or other gluten-free flour

1 cup [30 g] finely grated Parmigiano-Reggiano

4 Tbsp [60 ml] extra-virgin olive oil

8 corn tortillas, warmed

½ head red or green cabbage, cored and finely shredded

Lime wedges for serving

To make the mango salsa: Combine the mangos, onion, jalapeño (if using), lime juice, and cilantro in a bowl and stir to combine. Taste, adding salt and lime juice as desired. Set aside.

To make the avocado crema: Place the avocado flesh and ¼ tsp salt in a medium bowl. Using a fork or a pastry blender, mash until very smooth. Stir in the mayonnaise and lime juice. Taste, adding additional salt and lime juice as desired. (Store, with a piece of plastic wrap pressed directly onto the surface, in the refrigerator for up to 2 days.)

Rinse the tilapia and pat dry. Halve each fillet lengthwise by slicing down the middle seam. Season with salt and pepper. Whisk the eggs in a shallow bowl. Place the flour, Parmigiano-Reggiano, and ½ tsp salt in another small bowl and stir to combine. Dip the fish, one piece at a time, into the eggs, coating evenly and allowing any excess to drip off into the bowl. Then place in the flour mixture and coat both sides evenly, gently tapping off any excess. Arrange the coated fish on a baking sheet in a single layer.

Line another baking sheet with paper towels. In a large nonstick skillet over medium-high heat, warm 2 Tbsp of the olive oil. Working in two batches, place the fish pieces in the skillet and cook until golden brown on each side and opaque in the center, about 2 minutes per side. Transfer to the prepared sheet. Pour any remaining oil from the skillet, wipe clean with a paper towel, and add the remaining 2 Tbsp olive oil.

Spread some avocado crema on each tortilla. Top with cabbage, a piece of fish, and a spoonful of mango salsa. Serve with lime wedges and extra crema and salsa on the side.

CHICKEN CHILE VERDE

I have no idea why I don't use a slow cooker more often, since I'm always glad I can put everything in at night or before work, and let it do its magic. If you don't have a slow cooker, bake the chicken in a covered stockpot or Dutch oven for 1 to 1½ hours at 350°F [175°C]. If you are sensitive to nightshades, you could substitute chimichurri (see page 56) for the salsa verde.

PREPARATION TIME
15 minutes

COOKING TIME
2 hours 15 minutes

SERVES
4–6

8 bone-in, skin-on chicken thighs

Kosher salt

Freshly ground black pepper

2 Tbsp extra-virgin olive oil

½ cup [120 ml] chicken or vegetable stock

2 cups [460 g] Tomatillo and Jalapeño Salsa Verde (page 106) or other salsa verde

Rinse the chicken thighs and pat dry with paper towels. Season generously on both sides with salt and pepper.

In a large sauté pan over medium-high heat, warm the olive oil until just smoking. Working in batches, add the chicken thighs skin-side down and cook until the skin is golden brown and very crispy, 5 to 6 minutes. Turn, cooking the other side for 3 to 4 minutes, then transfer the chicken to a plate.

Once all the chicken thighs have been seared, pour off any accumulated fat and return the pan to medium-high heat. Add the chicken stock and salsa verde and bring to a boil, scraping up any browned bits from the bottom of the pan. Pour the mixture into a slow cooker and nestle the chicken thighs on top. Cover and cook until the chicken is fork-tender, about 2 hours on the high setting or about 4 hours on the low setting. Skim any excess fat off the surface before serving.

CHICKEN PHO

The first time I ever had pho was at the Slanted Door, Charles Phan's Vietnamese restaurant that has become a San Francisco Bay Area institution. I was blown away. The beauty of the dish lies in its simplicity. It requires a gentle coaxing of a few key ingredients—chicken or beef, onion, and ginger—to create a stock that is delicious on its own. I've tried a few of Phan's pho recipes, and the attention he spends bringing out all the flavors is incredible. In an effort to save time and eliminate hard-to-find ingredients, I offer my humble version. I've substituted brown rice noodles for the traditional rice noodles, and they've been a hit.

PREPARATION TIME
30 minutes

COOKING TIME
3 hours

SERVES
6

One 4- to 5-lb [1.8- to 2.3-kg] chicken, quartered, backbone reserved

2 yellow onions, peeled and halved

One 2-in [5-cm] piece fresh ginger, peeled and smashed

Kosher salt

2 tsp light brown sugar

5 qt [4.7 L] water

¼ cup [60 ml] fish sauce, plus more for serving

1 lb [455 g] dried brown rice noodles, such as Annie Chun's Pad Thai Brown Rice Noodles

1 bunch green onions, green parts only, thinly sliced

2 cups [120 g] mung bean sprouts

2 jalapeños, thinly sliced (optional if nightshade-sensitive)

Torn basil, cilantro, and mint leaves for serving

Lime wedges for serving

Sriracha sauce for serving (optional)

Place the chicken pieces and backbone, onions, ginger, 2 tsp salt, brown sugar, and water in a stockpot with at least an 8-qt [7.5-L] capacity. Slowly bring to a boil over medium-high heat. Turn the heat to medium-low and simmer gently, uncovered, for 1 hour, skimming off any impurities that come to the surface. (Add water as necessary to keep the chicken covered.)

Using tongs, remove the chicken pieces from the pot and transfer to a cutting board. When the chicken is cool to the touch, remove all the meat from the skin and bones and transfer to a medium bowl. Return the skin and bones to the stockpot. Shred the meat, then cover and refrigerate until ready to serve.

Return the stock to a simmer and continue to cook for 1½ to 2 hours. Using a fine-mesh sieve, strain the stock into another stockpot and cook over high heat until reduced to 12 cups [3 L], about 20 minutes. Stir in the fish sauce. (At this point, you can cool the stock to room temperature, cover, and refrigerate for up to 3 days.)

Prepare the rice noodles according to the package instructions.

While the noodles cook, add half of the shredded chicken to the stock and simmer until the chicken is warmed through. (Reserve the remaining shredded chicken for another use). Divide the cooked rice noodles among six large soup bowls and sprinkle evenly with the green onions, bean sprouts, and jalapeños (if using). Ladle the stock and chicken over the noodles and finish with the torn herbs. Serve with lime wedges, additional fish sauce, and Sriracha sauce, if desired.

a reliable option

When shopping in a typical grocery store with a limited assortment of Asian ingredients, I always turn to Annie Chun's for rice noodles and Thai Kitchen for guaranteed gluten-free fish sauce.

COUNTRY CAPTAIN'S CHICKEN

with curry and raisins

I thought my grandmother was the only one who knew about this recipe. Then I discovered its rich tradition in American history through Marion Cunningham, the author who completely revised and updated the classic *Fannie Farmer Cookbook*. The dish was created by people who settled in the Charleston-Savannah area of South Carolina, including people of Indian, Asian, and French descent (hence, the addition of the curry powder). The balance of sweet, salty, and spicy is phenomenal. If you are sensitive to nightshades, omit the tomato paste and diced tomatoes.

PREPARATION TIME
30 minutes

COOKING TIME
1 hour 10 minutes

SERVES
4–6

One 4- to 5-lb [1.8- to 2.3-kg] chicken, cut into 8 pieces

Kosher salt

2 Tbsp extra-virgin olive oil

1 large red onion, thinly sliced

3 celery stalks, sliced

1½ Tbsp curry powder

Freshly ground black pepper

2 Tbsp tomato paste (optional if nightshade-sensitive)

One 28-oz [800-g] can diced tomatoes (optional if nightshade-sensitive)

1 cup [240 ml] chicken or vegetable stock

½ cup [85 g] raisins

½ cup [65 g] raw almonds, toasted and coarsely chopped

4 cups [520 g] cooked brown rice

2 Tbsp chopped parsley

Rinse the chicken pieces and pat dry thoroughly. Season with salt.

In a large Dutch oven or stockpot over medium-high heat, warm the olive oil until just smoking. Working in batches, sear the chicken until well browned on both sides, 8 to 10 minutes per batch. Transfer the chicken to a platter and pour off all but 2 Tbsp of the accumulated fat. (If the bottom of the pot is scorched, discard the oil, wipe it clean, and add another 2 Tbsp oil.)

Turn the heat to medium and add the onion and celery. Cook, stirring frequently, until the onion is soft, 5 to 7 minutes. Add the curry powder, $\frac{1}{2}$ tsp black pepper, and tomato paste (if using) and cook, stirring constantly, until fragrant, about 30 seconds. Add the tomatoes with their juices (if using), chicken stock, and raisins and bring to a simmer, scraping the bottom of the pot to remove all the caramelized bits.

Nestle the chicken into the pot, cover, and turn the heat to medium-low. Simmer until chicken thighs are fork-tender, about 45 minutes.

Transfer the chicken to a platter, turn the heat to medium-high, and cook, stirring occasionally, until the sauce has reduced slightly, 5 to 7 minutes. Taste, adding more salt and pepper if necessary.

Stir the toasted almonds into the brown rice. Spoon on plates and top with the chicken and sauce. Finish with the parsley. Serve immediately.

make it ahead

Preparing this braise a day or two in advance will only enhance the flavors, making it the ideal dish for company or a wonderful make-ahead meal for a weeknight dinner. Once it cools, store it covered in the refrigerator in the pot you cooked it in. When it's time to reheat, place the covered Dutch oven over low heat. Stir after a few minutes, then cook until the meat is just warmed through, about 10 minutes.

LAMB BURGERS
with Pickled Onions and Herbed Yogurt Sauce

Lamb burgers once were something I liked to order when eating out but rarely prepared at home. Now I'm hooked on my homemade version. Loaded with fresh herbs and a few dried spices, the lamb mixture can be made ahead and kept in the refrigerator all day before cooking in a cast-iron skillet or on a grill. I use a little pork to mellow the lamb flavor and add some extra fat to the mixture. I skip the bun and serve the burgers on a bed of greens with herbed yogurt sauce, but the burgers can be served on traditional buns, if you like.

PREPARATION TIME
40 minutes
(plus 2 hours for pickling onions)

COOKING TIME
15 minutes

SERVES
6

PICKLED ONIONS

½ red onion, thinly sliced

6 Tbsp [90 ml] lime juice

½ tsp kosher salt

½ tsp raw cane sugar

HERBED YOGURT SAUCE

1 cup [230 g] Greek yogurt

2 Tbsp lemon juice

1 garlic clove, minced

2 Tbsp finely chopped mixed herbs such as dill, parsley, and mint

Kosher salt

CONTINUED

LAMB BURGERS

1 Tbsp olive oil

½ red onion, finely diced

1 lb [455 g] ground lamb

8 oz [230 g] ground pork

3 Tbsp finely chopped mint

2 Tbsp finely chopped dill

3 Tbsp finely chopped parsley

4 garlic cloves, minced

1½ tsp ground cumin

1 tsp ground coriander

1 tsp kosher salt

½ tsp freshly ground black pepper

Mixed greens, sliced tomatoes (optional if nightshade-sensitive), and sliced cucumbers for serving

To make the pickled onions: Place the onion, lime juice, salt, and sugar in a small bowl. Stir to combine, cover, and let sit at room temperature for about 2 hours to soften. Refrigerate until ready to use.

To make the herbed yogurt sauce: In a small bowl, stir together the yogurt, lemon juice, garlic, herbs, and ½ tsp salt. Adjust the salt to taste. Cover and refrigerate until ready to serve, or for up to 2 days.

To make the lamb burgers: In a small skillet over medium heat, warm the olive oil. Add the onion and cook, stirring frequently, until softened, about 7 minutes. Transfer to a small plate to cool.

In a large bowl, combine the lamb, pork, mint, dill, parsley, garlic, cumin, coriander, salt, pepper, and cooled onions. Gently mix with your hands. Do not overwork the meat. Divide the mixture into six equal balls. Press into patties and transfer to a parchment-lined baking sheet. (If not cooking immediately, cover and refrigerate for up to 8 hours.)

Heat a cast-iron skillet over medium-high heat until just smoking. Working in batches, sear the burgers until well browned, 2 to 3 minutes per side for medium-rare, or about 5 minutes per side for well-done. Alternatively, prepare a grill for cooking over medium-high heat. Lightly grease the grill grate. Place the burgers on the grill, and cook, turning once, to reach desired doneness, about 3 minutes per side for medium-rare, or about 5 minutes per side for well-done.

Transfer the burgers to a plate to rest for 5 minutes before serving. Top with a generous dollop of herbed yogurt sauce and some pickled onions. Add greens and sliced tomatoes or cucumbers. Serve immediately.

how to season burger patties

Seasoning meat well is so important. Many times we under- or overseason, then cook the meat and are left with no chance of improving it. Before shaping my patties, I heat a small skillet and cook a test patty, about 1 in [2.5 cm] in diameter, to check for flavor. I adjust the salt and spices if necessary before I form all the patties and cook them.

BIBIMBAP

I'm bibimbap obsessed. Sandra Wu, one of the test-kitchen cooks at Williams-Sonoma, made it for lunch one day after learning I'd never had it. When I looked in the bowl, I realized everything was really good for me. I tweaked her version to amp up the healthful factor. Gochujang is fermented Korean chile paste; you will find it at your local Asian foods market.

PREPARATION TIME
40 minutes
(plus 30 inactive)

COOKING TIME
30 minutes

SERVES
4

8 oz [230 g] flank steak, thinly sliced across the grain

6½ tsp tamari

2 tsp minced garlic

3 tsp toasted sesame oil

2½ tsp raw cane sugar

9 tsp organic canola oil

½ yellow onion, thinly sliced

1 carrot, peeled and julienned

Kosher salt

1 red bell pepper, seeded and cut into thin strips (optional if nightshade-sensitive)

2 small crookneck squash or zucchini, cut into ¼-in [6-mm] matchsticks

8 oz [230 g] baby spinach

8 oz [230 g] mung bean sprouts

1 Tbsp sesame seeds

8 oz [230 g] shiitake mushrooms, stemmed and thinly sliced

4 cups [800 g] steamed short-grain brown rice

4 fried eggs

Kimchi and gochujang for serving

CONTINUED

In a medium bowl, combine the steak with 4½ tsp of the tamari, 1 tsp of the garlic, 1 tsp of the sesame oil, and 2 tsp of the sugar. Marinate at room temperature for 30 minutes.

In a large nonstick skillet over medium-high heat, warm 1 tsp of the canola oil. Add the onion and carrot, season with salt, and cook, stirring occasionally, until tender-crisp, 4 to 6 minutes. Transfer to a medium bowl.

Repeat the process to cook each vegetable separately until just tender, seasoning each with a pinch of salt and adding it to the onion and carrot when done. Cook the bell pepper in 1 tsp canola oil; the squash in 1 tsp canola oil and 1 tsp sesame oil; the spinach in 1 tsp canola oil, adding the remaining 1 tsp garlic during the last minute of cooking; and the bean sprouts and sesame seeds in 1 tsp canola oil and the remaining 1 tsp sesame oil.

Add 2 tsp canola oil to the skillet. Add the mushrooms and cook until browned, about 5 minutes. Add the remaining 2 tsp tamari and remaining ½ tsp sugar and cook until glazed, about 1 minute. Transfer to the bowl of vegetables.

Add the remaining 2 tsp canola oil to the skillet, turn the heat to high, add the steak, and cook until browned on both sides, 3 to 4 minutes.

Divide the rice among four bowls. Top evenly with the meat and vegetables, followed by a fried egg. Serve with kimchi and gochujang.

easier than it looks

Though this recipe may look intimidating, it's all about your prep work and being organized. Use the time when the steak is marinating to prep the vegetables and start the rice. Keep in mind that bibimbap is customizable. If you want to leave out the steak for a vegetarian option or remove one of the vegetables, feel free, but I highly recommend keeping the fried egg. Along with the kimchi and gochujang, the runny yolk creates a delicious sauce when mixed with the other ingredients.

GRILLED RIB-EYE AND SUMMER SUCCOTASH

with lime-herb vinaigrette

Cattle raised strictly on grass have a different fat composition than those fed grain. Meat from grass-fed cattle is rich in omega-3 and omega-6 fatty acids, the types found in salmon and other oily fish. The key to including beef in your diet is portion control. A 4-oz [115-g] portion of grass-fed beef every once in a while can be healthful. This succotash includes a bounty of summer vegetables, but you can certainly adapt it, removing nightshades and replacing them with additional edamame, fava beans, or any other favorite vegetable.

PREPARATION TIME
45 minutes
(plus 1 hour for steak to rest before cooking)

COOKING TIME
20 minutes

SERVES
4

One 1-lb [455-g] boneless rib-eye steak

Olive oil for brushing

Kosher salt

Freshly ground black pepper

1 small shallot, minced

3 Tbsp lime juice

1 Tbsp sherry vinegar

1 Tbsp Dijon mustard

1 Tbsp honey

1/4 cup [60 ml] extra-virgin olive oil

3 Tbsp finely chopped herbs, such as basil, mint, and chives

3 zucchini, ends trimmed, sliced lengthwise into strips 1/2 in [12 mm] thick

2 summer squash, ends trimmed, sliced lengthwise into strips 1/2 in [12 mm] thick

2 red or yellow bell peppers, halved and seeds, core, and stem removed (optional if nightshade-sensitive)

2 cups [280 g] cherry tomatoes, halved (optional if nightshade-sensitive)

1 cup [150 g] edamame, fava beans, or other shelled fresh beans, blanched

CONTINUED

Rinse the steak and thoroughly pat dry. Place on a plate and brush both sides with olive oil. Season generously with salt and pepper and let rest at room temperature for 1 hour.

In a small bowl, whisk together the shallot, lime juice, vinegar, mustard, and honey. Slowly whisk in the extra-virgin olive oil to form a vinaigrette. Gently stir in the herbs, then taste and season with salt and pepper. Set aside.

Prepare a grill for direct cooking over high heat.

Brush the zucchini strips, summer squash strips, and bell pepper halves on both sides with olive oil, then sprinkle with salt and pepper. Grill the zucchini and squash until just cooked through, about 2 minutes per side. Transfer to a cutting board. Grill the bell peppers, turning occasionally, until charred and blistered, 5 to 7 minutes. Place in a small bowl and cover with plastic wrap. Allow the vegetables to cool.

While the vegetables cool, grill the steak until well seared and an instant-read thermometer inserted into the center reads 130°F [55°C] for medium-rare, 3 to 4 minutes per side, or grill longer to reach the desired doneness. Allow the steak to rest on a cutting board for 5 to 10 minutes before slicing across the grain.

Remove the skins from the cooled bell peppers. Cut the zucchini, squash, and peppers into ½-in [12-mm] dice. Place the vegetables in a large bowl and add the tomatoes (if using) and edamame. Pour half of the vinaigrette over the vegetables and toss to coat, adjusting with more vinaigrette as desired.

Place several generous spoonsful of the succotash on each plate, then pair with a fourth of the sliced steak. Serve immediately.

room temperature matters

When cooking proteins like beef and pork, it's imperative to remove the meat from the refrigerator an hour before cooking. Letting it come to room temperature ensures that it will cook evenly, no matter which temperature you prefer. In addition, rest the cooked meat for 10 minutes before slicing. This allows the juices to be reabsorbed into the meat instead of being lost on the cutting board.

chapter

6

DESSERTS

Outside my home, we face a daily assault of sugar, from treats handed out by well-meaning parents at sports games to coworkers' birthdays and ice-cream socials at the office. My philosophy on allowing sugar is moderation. We don't have sweet treats every night in my house, but when we do, I want them to be really satisfying. I prefer to prepare sweets myself for a few reasons: I use the minimal amount of sugar possible to make them taste great, I can manage the portion control, and I love how happy everyone is to have a dessert made from scratch. So when you feel like indulging in a sweet treat, these are my go-to choices. Every recipe here is better for you than its commercially made equivalent or the packaged treat you might choose instead.

BLACKBERRIES AND BLUEBERRIES
with whipped goat cheese

Dark berries are full of antioxidants, and research shows that blueberries can even improve memory. Serving the berries with this whipped goat cheese always wows dinner guests. Since it's so thick and creamy, I like to put a little in the bottom of a bowl or wineglass, add the berries, and then top with a bit more whipped cheese. Kudos to recipe tester Amanda Frederickson for creating this goat cheese and honey combo.

PREPARATION TIME

10 minutes
(plus 20 minutes for goat cheese to soften)

SERVES

4

5 oz [140 g] goat cheese, at room temperature

1½ Tbsp honey, plus more for serving

1 Tbsp lemon juice

½ tsp grated orange zest

Kosher salt

2 cups [240 g] blueberries

2 cups [240 g] blackberries

¼ cup [30 g] pistachios, chopped

Place the goat cheese, honey, lemon juice, orange zest, and a pinch of salt in a medium bowl. Whisk until the goat cheese is fluffy and smooth.

Divide the goat cheese mixture among bowls or wineglasses, reserving about four spoonsful. Top each portion with berries, pistachios, and a spoonful of the whipped goat cheese. Drizzle with additional honey. Serve immediately.

anything goes

Use any kind of fruit for this dessert. And if you are feeling adventurous, fold in your favorite jam or lemon curd for an extra-special treat.

LIME SORBET

This sorbet (pictured on page 177, bottom) literally wakes me up when I eat it. Many traditional recipes use a simple syrup of equal parts water and sugar given the tartness of limes, but I reduce the sugar by half, which allows the lime flavor to shine. If you're preparing a multicourse meal, you could serve the sorbet as the palate cleanser after an especially rich second or third course. For a mojito-style twist, mix a little chopped mint in with the lime juice.

PREPARATION TIME

10 minutes
(plus 20 to 30 minutes in ice-cream maker and 3 hours in freezer)

SERVES

4

1 cup [240 ml] water

½ cup [100 g] raw cane sugar

1 cup [240 ml] lime juice, plus grated zest from ½ lime

Fill a medium bowl with ice water. Combine the 1 cup [240 ml] water and sugar in a small saucepan. Warm over low heat until the sugar is dissolved. Remove the simple syrup from the heat, place the pan in the ice-water bath, and stir to chill rapidly. Alternatively, refrigerate the syrup until chilled, about 3 hours. (Store in an airtight container in the refrigerator for up to 2 weeks.)

Combine the lime juice with 1 cup [240 ml] of the simple syrup in a medium bowl. Whisk in the lime zest. Freeze the sorbet in an ice-cream maker according to the manufacturer's instructions. Transfer the ice cream to a freezer-safe container and place in the freezer for 3 hours to set, or store for up to 2 weeks.

STRAWBERRY-LIME GRANITA

This granita (pictured opposite, top) is basically a frozen version of my favorite agua fresca flavor. It has clean, bright flavors, and with the strawberries and limes, it has a double dose of vitamin C.

PREPARATION TIME
1 hour 45 minutes

SERVES
4–6

1 cup [240 ml] water

½ cup [100 g] raw cane sugar

1 lb [455 g] strawberries, stems removed

½ cup [120 ml] lime juice

Fill a medium bowl with ice water. Combine the 1 cup [240 ml] water and sugar in a small saucepan. Warm over low heat until the sugar is dissolved. Remove the simple syrup from the heat, place the pan in the ice-water bath, and stir to chill rapidly. Alternatively, refrigerate the syrup until chilled, about 3 hours. (Store in an airtight container in the refrigerator for up to 2 weeks.)

Reserve four to six strawberries for garnish. Place the remaining strawberries in a blender or food processor. Blend until smooth, then strain through a fine-mesh sieve into a medium bowl to remove the seeds.

Add the lime juice and ½ cup [120 ml] of the simple syrup to the strawberry juice. Stir and taste, adding more simple syrup if desired.

Pour the strawberry mixture into a 13-by-9-by-2-in [33-by-23-by-5-cm] non-stick metal baking pan. Freeze until the mixture is icy around the edges, about 25 minutes. Using a fork, stir the icy portions into the middle of the pan. Continue this process of stirring the icy edges into center every 25 minutes for about 1½ hours, or until the mixture has turned into flaky crystals. Cover tightly and freeze for up to 1 day.

To serve, scrape the granita into serving bowls or glasses and garnish with the reserved berries.

CHOCOLATE-CINNAMON GELATO

If I had my way, I'd eat gelato daily. So I set out to develop a version that's better for me. I've reduced the amount of sugar that is typically used and opted for dark chocolate for a heart-healthy boost. Using almond milk instead of cow's milk means it works for everyone who can't tolerate dairy. The texture is similar to ice milk. Nostalgic!

PREPARATION TIME
15 minutes
(plus 20 to 30 minutes in ice-cream maker and 3 hours in freezer)

SERVES
4–6

2 tsp cornstarch

3 cups [720 ml] Almond Milk (page 68) or whole milk

¼ cup [50 g] raw cane sugar

¼ tsp kosher salt

4 oz [115 g] dark chocolate (70 percent cacao), coarsely chopped

1 tsp ground cinnamon

½ tsp vanilla extract

Chocolate shavings, crushed walnuts, or crushed fresh raspberries for garnish

Put the cornstarch in a small bowl, add 1 Tbsp of the almond milk, and stir with a fork to dissolve the cornstarch.

Pour the rest of the almond milk into a medium saucepan. Bring to a simmer over medium heat, then turn the heat to low. Whisk in the cornstarch mixture, sugar, and salt to dissolve. Add the chocolate and cinnamon and whisk until the mixture is completely smooth. Cook, whisking occasionally, until the mixture starts to thicken, about 5 minutes.

Pour the milk mixture through a fine-mesh strainer into a large bowl. Stir in the vanilla. Refrigerate until chilled, about 3 hours.

Whisk the chilled mixture. Freeze in an ice-cream maker according to the manufacturer's instructions. When ready, the gelato should be the consistency of soft-serve ice cream. Transfer to an airtight container and freeze for up to 1 week.

To serve, scoop into serving bowls and garnish as desired.

VEGAN CHOCOLATE POTS DE CRÈME

As I started to learn about anti-inflammation diets, I discovered that non-GMO soy is a wonderful source of protein and an excellent alternative to saturated fats. But I had never found a clever way to use silken tofu until I made this recipe. Served immediately, it's silky smooth. Chilled overnight, it's like an ultra-thick pot de crème. You won't believe how easy this is.

PREPARATION TIME
15 minutes

COOKING TIME
5 minutes

SERVES
4–6

1 lb [455 g] silken tofu, drained

2 tsp vanilla extract

Kosher salt

1½ cups [250 g] semisweet vegan chocolate chips

1 tsp maple syrup (optional)

Chopped strawberries or blueberries for garnish

In a medium saucepan, bring 2 in [5 cm] water to a simmer.

Place the tofu, vanilla, and ¼ tsp salt in a blender and puree on low speed until smooth, scraping down the sides with a spatula if needed.

When the water is simmering, place the chocolate chips in a medium heatproof bowl that will fit in the saucepan over the simmering water without touching it. Turn the heat to low and melt the chocolate, stirring, until smooth, 2 to 3 minutes.

Allow the chocolate to cool slightly, then pour into the blender. Puree until smooth, scraping down the sides if necessary, until the tofu and chocolate are combined. Taste and add the maple syrup if desired. Taste once more and add a pinch of salt if needed.

Divide the mixture evenly among six ½-cup [120-ml] ramekins. Garnish with berries before serving.

HONEY PANNA COTTA
with Blackberry-Lime Sauce

Panna cotta means "cooked cream" in Italian and has always been one of my favorite desserts. The luscious texture makes for the most elegant finish to a meal, and everyone thinks this dessert is more complicated than it is. Since I try not to eat a lot of dairy, I gave coconut milk a chance. The results? A delectably simple, smooth panna cotta with a dreamy texture. The blackberry-lime sauce is insanely appealing. You can substitute any berry that is readily available.

PREPARATION TIME	COOKING TIME	SERVES
10 minutes	5 minutes (plus 4 to 8 hours to set)	6

2½ cups [600 ml] canned unsweetened coconut milk

2 tsp gelatin

¼ cup [60 ml] honey

1 vanilla bean, split and seeds scraped

Kosher salt

BLACKBERRY-LIME SAUCE

2 cups [240 g] blackberries

Finely grated zest of ½ lime, plus 2 tsp lime juice

1 tsp raw cane sugar

Place ½ cup [120 ml] of the coconut milk in a small bowl. Sprinkle the gelatin over the top and allow it to sit for about 2 minutes.

Place the remaining 2 cups [480 ml] coconut milk, the honey, vanilla bean and its seeds, and a pinch of salt in a medium saucepan. Warm over low heat, whisking occasionally, until bubbles form around the edge of the pan. Remove from the heat and let the mixture steep for 5 minutes.

CONTINUED

Pour the coconut milk mixture through a fine-mesh strainer into a large bowl. Discard the vanilla bean. Whisk the gelatin mixture slowly into the warm coconut mixture until there are no lumps of gelatin. Divide evenly among six $\frac{1}{2}$-cup [120-ml] ramekins or wineglasses. Cover and refrigerate until set, at least 4 hours or up to overnight.

To make the blackberry-lime sauce: Place the blackberries, lime zest, lime juice, and sugar in a medium bowl. Using a fork or pastry blender, gently mash the berries, leaving some large pieces of berry while allowing some of the juices to make a sauce. Set aside for at least 10 minutes, or cover and refrigerate up to overnight.

Spoon the sauce over each chilled panna cotta. Serve immediately.

ALMOND-PISTACHIO LEMON CAKE
with Citrus Salad and Coconut Whipped Cream

You will never guess that this stunning finale to a meal doesn't include gluten or dairy. I owe the improvements to the talented Amanda Frederickson, who took my favorite version of almond-citrus cake and turned it into this masterpiece. The almonds and pistachios may be calorie laden, but they are loaded with magnesium and potassium, and they make a fantastic substitute for refined white flour.

PREPARATION TIME
30 minutes

COOKING TIME
40–45 minutes

SERVES
6–8

CAKE

1¼ cup [200 g] raw almonds or almond meal

½ cup [70 g] pistachios

½ tsp salt

6 eggs, separated

1¼ cup [250 g] raw cane sugar

1 Tbsp grated lemon zest

1 tsp grated orange zest

1 tsp vanilla extract

¼ tsp almond extract

COCONUT WHIPPED CREAM

One 13½-oz [400-ml] can full-fat coconut milk

1 Tbsp confectioner's sugar (optional)

CONTINUED

CITRUS SALAD

2 oranges, sectioned (see page 121)
2 grapefruits, sectioned (see page 121)
1 Tbsp mint leaves, cut into strips
1 Tbsp honey, plus more as needed

To make the cake: Preheat the oven to 350°F [180°C]. Coat a 9-in [23-cm] round springform pan with nonstick cooking spray.

In a food processor, combine the almonds, pistachios, and salt and pulse until finely ground. In a large bowl, combine the egg yolks and 1 cup [200 g] of the raw cane sugar. Beat until light and fluffy, about 2 minutes. Add the lemon zest, orange zest, vanilla, and almond extract and beat until incorporated.

In the clean bowl of a stand mixer fitted with the whisk attachment, beat the egg whites and the remaining ¼ cup [50 g] raw cane sugar on high speed until glossy, stiff peaks form.

Using a spatula, alternate folding the egg whites and the almond mixture into the egg yolk mixture, starting and ending with the egg whites. Pour into the prepared pan. Bake until a toothpick inserted into the center of the cake comes out clean and the top is golden brown, 40 to 45 minutes. Allow the cake to cool completely.

To make the coconut whipped cream: Chill the can of coconut milk, upside down, in the refrigerator overnight. Turn right-side up and open the can with a can opener. The water will be on the top. Carefully pour out the water and reserve for another use, so that only the coconut cream remains. Place the cream in a stand mixer fitted with the whisk attachment. Add the confectioner's sugar (if using) and whip on high speed until light and fluffy, 3 to 4 minutes.

To make the citrus salad: Combine the orange and grapefruit sections with the mint and honey in a medium bowl. Taste for sweetness and add more honey if needed.

Remove the sides of the springform pan and transfer the cake to a serving platter. Spread the coconut cream into an even layer over the cake. Cut the cake into wedges, then top with the citrus salad and serve.

CHOCOLATE-COCONUT BROWNIES

My son Charlie and I like to bake together. It makes baking feel special, and we enjoy our homemade treats more. I love that cocoa powder can replace a lot of the refined flour in brownies. Using coconut oil instead of butter gives these brownies a silky smooth texture while adding the health benefits of lauric acid, potentially lowering our LDL cholesterol. Eaten fresh out of the oven, these are ooey-gooey amazing. If you let them sit overnight, the brownies become firmer.

PREPARATION TIME
15 minutes

COOKING TIME
30–35 minutes

MAKES
16 brownies

½ cup [80 g] gluten-free flour, such as Cup4Cup or Bob's Red Mill

¼ cup [30 g] unsweetened alkalized cocoa powder

½ tsp sea salt

4 oz [115 g] semisweet chocolate, coarsely chopped

¾ cup [120 g] unrefined coconut oil

1 cup [200 g] raw cane sugar

4 eggs

1 tsp vanilla

4 oz [115 g] semisweet chocolate chips (optional)

Preheat the oven to 350°F [180°C]. Grease a 9-by-9-in [23-by-23-cm] baking pan and line with parchment paper.

Combine the flour, cocoa powder, and salt in a medium bowl. Set aside.

In a double boiler or microwave, melt the chopped chocolate and coconut oil. Let cool slightly. Add the sugar, eggs, and vanilla, whisking until well combined. Whisk in the flour mixture. Fold in the chocolate chips (if using). Pour into the prepared pan. Bake until a toothpick inserted in the center of the brownies comes out clean, 20 to 25 minutes. This will yield a somewhat gooey brownie. Continue to bake for 5 to 10 minutes if you prefer a drier brownie.

Let the brownies cool completely, then cut into squares. Store in an airtight container at room temperature for up to 3 days.

SEASONAL FRUIT CRISPS
with oatmeal crumble crust

When I bake my favorite crisp in ramekins so everyone can have their own, it feels as if we are at a fancy restaurant. So little effort with such outstanding results. Using ripe, juicy fruit provides enough natural sugar that you don't need to add much, if any, to the filling. Just look for whatever is in season—apples and pears in fall, berries in spring, stone fruits in summer. The heavy dose of oats in the topping provides a nutritional upgrade on the flour.

PREPARATION TIME
30 minutes

COOKING TIME
30–40 minutes
(plus 20 minutes to cool)

SERVES
8

---

2 cups [200 g] rolled oats

1½ cups [180 g] gluten-free flour, such as Cup4Cup or Bob's Red Mill, or all-purpose flour

---

¾ cup [150 g] firmly packed brown sugar

½ tsp ground cinnamon

¼ tsp ground nutmeg

¼ tsp kosher salt

½ cup [110 g] unsalted butter, cut into 8 pieces

---

2 to 3 lb [910 g to 1.4 kg] apples or pears, peeled, cored, and chopped, or other seasonal fruit

---

1 to 2 tsp raw cane sugar

Greek yogurt for serving

Honey for serving

Preheat the oven to 350°F [180°C]. Line a baking sheet with parchment paper, and place eight 1-cup [240-ml] ramekins on the prepared sheet.

Combine the oats, flour, brown sugar, cinnamon, nutmeg, and salt in a large bowl. Add the butter and use a pastry blender or fork to cut it into pea-size pieces. Refrigerate until ready to use.

Place the fruit in a medium bowl and taste, adding the raw cane sugar only if necessary to sweeten. Fill each ramekin to the top with fruit, then sprinkle with 3 Tbsp of the oat mixture. Bake until the tops are brown and bubbly, 30 to 40 minutes. Set aside to cool for 20 minutes.

Top with a dollop of Greek yogurt, drizzle with honey, and serve.

make the topping ahead

The topping for the crisp freezes well in an airtight container or freezer bag, so make a big batch and bring it out whenever you're in the mood for dessert.

INDEX